Do Not Go Gentle

A Memoir of Love, Loss, and Living On

Do Not Go Gentle

A Memoir of Love, Loss, and Living On

by Marcia Sartwell

Copyright © 2011 Marcia Sartwell

All rights reserved. No part of this book may be reproduced in whole or in part without written permission from the author, except by reviewers who may quote excerpts in connection with a review in a newspaper, magazine, or electronic publication.

The editorial, "Behind the Lines," first appeared in the June 1980 issue of *Defenders* magazine and is reprinted by permission of Defenders of Wildlife.

Cover photo: Marcia Sartwell. All other photos are by Frank Sartwell or the author.

ISBN: 1463703457
ISBN-13: 9781463703455

In Memory of
Frank Sartwell

Do not go gentle into that good night.
Rage, rage against the dying of the light.
Dylan Thomas, Do Not Go Gentle Into That Good Night

Do not go gentle into that good night.
Rage, rage against the dying of the light.
Dylan Thomas, Do Not Go Gentle Into That Good Night

Acknowledgments

It seems a long time ago that I began to write this book. Many people have helped me along the way. I am grateful to Mayanne Karmin, who had faith in this project when mine had faltered and whose skillful editorial work in an earlier version brought many lasting improvements. I wish also to thank Carolyn Shank, M.S.W., who guided me through dark places into brighter ones and helped make the affirmative epilogue possible. My greatest debt is to Cathy Baker, whose sensitive editing and literary judgment have been invaluable and without whose steady support I would never have completed this book.

Contents

Preface xiii

Chapter 1 *Confused Alarms* 1

Chapter 2 *Come Live with Me* 9

Chapter 3 *Earth Can Be So Sweet* 21

Chapter 4 *Master of Fantasy* 35

Chapter 5 *Tho' Much Is Taken* 41

Chapter 6 *A Ceaseless Rain* 47

Chapter 7 *To Undo Things Done* 55

Chapter 8 *The Shadow of Death* 65

Chapter 9 *The Wine Cup of This Fury* 75

Chapter 10 *A Calmer Grief* 85

Chapter 11 *Surprised by Joy* 95

Chapter 12 *Break, Break, Break* 101

Chapter 13 *Butterflies Are Forever* 109

Chapter 14 *A Narrow Time* 119

Epilogue 129

Preface

Many years ago, when my husband, 49 years old, became gravely ill, I felt a sense of shock and disbelief that our life together would soon be over. In spite of my sadness, I wanted with all my heart not just to make the best use of the time we had left together but to be the perfect partner—selfless, uncomplaining, cheerful. Yet within six months I was struggling desperately. My moods swung from loving and tender one moment to irritable, angry, or despairing the next. I thought I must be the only person in the world to have such terrible feelings, and I searched in vain for a book that could help me understand what I was going through and, I hoped, tell me that what I felt was not despicable but human. No such book existed then, or, if it did, I could not find it.

I did not set out then to write such a book. Writing, though, was one of the ways I survived. My husband had chosen to face his illness by denying that it was serious. Until almost the day he died, he insisted that he would be well one day, and he wanted me to express the same kind of optimism. Since I could not be honest with him, I put my thoughts and feelings into a journal, where at least I could be honest with myself. After he died, I realized that I had the basis for the kind of book I had once sought—an honest book about how it felt to be the caregiver of a dying husband.

The journal captures the raw emotion of the moment—too raw, as it turned out, for some of my friends. Several of them read it and considered parts of it shocking. I accepted their judgment and put the manuscript in the back of a file cabinet drawer, where it stayed for twenty years.

When I finally took it out and looked at it again, I decided there is more in it to comfort than to shock. While there are passages of anguish that may still jolt, I think that readers today are much more accustomed to honest expressions of feeling. And while the passage of time has made some of the details obsolete (you can't buy a waterfront lot in Chincoteague for $18,000 anymore, and no doubt the medicines for treating COPD have changed), the workings of the human heart under stress remain the same.

There are many good books on death and dying, but it seems to me that the role of the caregiver, caught up in these final events, has not been sufficiently explored. The experience is so common. A spouse becomes terminally ill. The partner is plunged into a new role as primary caregiver—the one who tries every day to ease the process of dying, who lives with the certainty of loss and the uncertainty of when, and who must deal with all the unfamiliar problems that come up.

Few are prepared for the task; most go into it armed only with good intentions. Yet seeing a spouse through to the end makes enormous demands on the caregiver—physical stamina, emotional resilience, self-sacrifice. It can be a traumatic experience—one that brings unexpected and unwanted feelings. I hope that this book may help other care-givers feel less lonely as they grapple with their own feelings in watching a loved one die.

Aside from a few names that have been changed, everything in the book is true. Nothing has been fictionalized to make the picture prettier or the narrator nicer. The conversations recorded here did occur. The journal entries have not been rewritten, however stark they may be at times.

I am pleased now that I did not publish this book when I first wrote it, for at that time I felt that my life was over, that even though I might go on living, I would never again be happy. I was wrong. In an epilogue I have sketched out my life since my husband died. Though scarcely a day passes that I do not think of him, I have not just survived; I have found life rich in meaning and frequently joyful. I hope that readers will find consolation in knowing that it is possible to go through a prolonged period of desolation and despair and still survive intact; and that if we do not close our hearts, the experience will give us an understanding and an appreciation of life that we did not have before.

Marcia Sartwell
Bethesda, Maryland
July 1, 2011

CHAPTER 1
Confused Alarms

> And we are here as on a darkling plain
> Swept with confused alarms.
>
> Matthew Arnold, *Dover Beach*

It was four o'clock on a cold morning in March 1978, and for hours I had lain sleepless, listening to the rasping sounds of my husband's breathing. Slowly the anxiety I'd felt for weeks turned to full-blown alarm. I could bear it no longer. I pulled on a bathrobe, tromped downstairs, and made some coffee. Then I sat down by the telephone and waited for the world to wake up so I could do what I should have done weeks before.

Frank was very ill; I was sure of it—even if I couldn't prove it, even if he didn't admit it, even if the doctor was not concerned. Suddenly I didn't care how adamantly Frank refused to go to the hospital or how reassuring the doctor was. I knew in that moment that I could override both of them.

As I waited, I asked myself over and over how this had happened. Only six weeks ago Frank had seemed so well. Yes, I knew that thirty years of smoking three packs of cigarettes a day had taken their toll on his lungs. He had quit smoking more than a year ago, though—right after we married—and the results had been dramatic. The terrible cough cleared up. His color improved. He had more energy. The doctor was very pleased. We all were.

He had even recovered from the flu faster than anyone else. It had been a family joke about how we spent our first anniversary recovering from the flu. Frank came down with it a few days after Christmas; then I caught it; and then my son, Dan, home from college for the holidays, came down with it. "We had a real pest house going there for awhile," Frank wrote to a friend, "with whoever was least sick pouring chicken soup for the rest of us." But Frank had recovered quickly. The only hitch—and it seemed minor—was that he was allergic to one of the prescribed drugs, ampicillin. He had broken out in purple blotches, and it had taken several weeks on a drug called prednisone before they disappeared completely. Even with the rash, though, he clearly felt well. I'd never seen him move so fast or do so much.

So, what had happened? Why had he started to feel so bad in early February? Overnight, the things he used to do left him breathless. And why didn't Dr. McMinn (not his real name) do something? He hadn't seemed on top of the situation since that scene in his office a month ago. I'd been in the waiting room expecting that after the exam Frank would call me in, as usual, for a talk with the doctor. Suddenly he burst out of the office, shirt unbuttoned and shirttail out, jammed his feet into his galoshes, and grabbed his coat.

"Let's get out of here," he said.

"What's wrong?"

"I'll tell you about it in the car." His unbuckled galoshes flapped around his ankles as he raced for the elevator.

As we pulled out of the parking garage, Frank explained, "He wanted to put me in the hospital."

"That's probably where you ought to be."

"I knew you'd be on his side."

"I'm not on his side. Why won't you go?"

"You don't go to the hospital unless you are terribly sick. I am not terribly sick. He can treat me at home."

I was doubtful, but he was determined and, wanting to believe him, I went along. Thus began three weeks of doctoring him at home—phone calls that resulted in adjustments to the medication, office visits that did the same. Once the doctor ran some tests. In a few days he phoned to say the lab reports had come in and everything looked fine (Whose lab tests did the doctor have, I wondered later). And all the while it seemed to me that Frank was getting worse. Now if he walked from the kitchen table to the sink for a glass of water, he had to lean against the sink to catch his breath.

"Frank, call the doctor," I pleaded. "Tell him how you are."

Once he did call. I overheard part of the conversation. "Not so bad, doctor. How's yourself?"

Frank never did level with the doctor. It baffled me. Perhaps if we had been married longer, I would have understood him better—would have known that he couldn't tell the doctor what he wouldn't admit to himself. I'd have known that this most intelligent man, formerly the writer of a medical column and the editor of *Science* magazine, was playing a game of sheer fantasy: "If I don't admit it, it won't be true. If I don't go to a hospital, I can't really be sick."

But I didn't understand it then. I'd taken to phoning the doctor secretly from the office to say that Frank was worse than he admitted. That is, I'd done it until the doctor informed me coolly, "You know, Mrs. Sartwell, you don't really need to phone. Your husband and I know much more about how he feels than you do." Feeling thoroughly put down and somewhat humiliated, I stopped phoning. For the next week I just stood by, numb with anxiety. Until now. Now I knew what to do, and I would not be derailed by the doctor or by Frank.

It was getting light. I went upstairs, dressed, and packed Frank's bag for the hospital. At eight o'clock I phoned the doctor. No, I told the nurse, I did not want the doctor to return my call. This was an emergency: I must talk with him now. The doctor came to the phone.

I announced my intention to take Frank to the hospital that morning. "Which one do you want him in and when can you be there?"

"He won't go."

"Oh, yes, he will," I said, with a new edge in my voice.

"I'll phone Georgetown Hospital for a room and meet you there at ten."

Then I woke Frank, fixed his breakfast, and told him.

"Are you sure..."

"I'm sure."

"Maybe it's a good idea." I think he was glad that I was taking over. Getting things done was becoming easy now that I trusted my own judgment.

He was admitted through the emergency room, and very quickly a resident came to take his medical history. Name: Frank Sartwell. Age: 49. Occupation: Editor of *Defenders* magazine. Organization: Defenders of Wildlife, Washington, DC.

Dr. McMinn arrived, looking cheerful.

"Patient is completely breathless with minimal effort," said the resident. Other doctors came in, talked, probed, consulted, and soon solved the mystery of what had gone wrong. Frank had never recovered from the flu. The prednisone, prescribed for the rash, had cleared up the rash all right, but it had masked the symptoms of a lung infection, the product of the flu. Throughout January and half of February, while he was on prednisone, Frank felt just fine. He forgot about the flu. The doctor forgot about the flu, too, unfortunately. When Frank came off prednisone in mid-February, he immediately began suffering the effects of the lung infection, which had been there all along, destroying lung tissue.

Oh, God, I thought as the doctors were explaining all this. How much damage has been done?

Doctors often don't answer direct questions like that with direct answers. They do not want to predict the course of an illness, nor do they want to take away your hope. So they talk to you about the improvements in drugs, the benefits of lung therapy, and the importance of a positive attitude. You learn to listen carefully to their answers, noting which questions they answer and which ones they evade. In time you learn more from the evasions.

A couple of days later, quite by accident, I got some answers. I had come to the hospital after work to visit Frank, who was then the only patient in a double room. Georgetown is a teaching hospital, and eight medical students circled the bed, where a doctor was demonstrating a new instrument for measuring lung capacity. I slipped unnoticed into a chair at the dark end of the room.

"Blow as hard as you can into this tube," the doctor instructed Frank.

"This can't be right," he told his students moments later as he read the results. "That reading is much too low. When the patient catches his breath, we'll try again."

A few moments later, he tried again.

"That's even worse. I didn't know. . . ." He paused. "Maybe there is something wrong with the instrument."

Hurriedly, followed by his entourage, he scurried out of the room. And as I looked at the exhausted man lying back on the pillows, I knew there was nothing wrong with the doctor's instrument.

For a moment the room spun wildly, and I had a sensation of whirling into an abyss. I put my head down and forced myself to open my eyes and concentrate on something. There, on the black and white tiles of the hospital floor, were my blue shoes with the square brass buckles. The feet in the shoes were mine. I wasn't falling. I was sitting, cold and damp with sweat, in a chair in a hospital room. I stared at my shoes until the room held still again.

My first clear thought pierced like a knife. I had brought him here too late. I was the only one who had seen what was happening, and I had acted too late.

I could not face what I knew. With the logic of desperation, I fought knowing it: It can't be true, I told myself. It can't be true because I couldn't bear it if it were.

Then I found more logical grounds for rejecting it: What did I know about that test? Not a thing. Maybe a low score didn't mean anything. Maybe there really was something wrong with the instrument.

In a few minutes I went over to his bed. "Hi, Frank."

"I thought you'd never get here."

"The traffic held me up. How are you feeling?"

"Much better," he said with a wan smile. Until a few weeks before he died, Frank always reported himself "much better," a response that confused quite a few people who were not used to his subterfuges. "They took some tubes out today, so I've got an arm free for hugging you. Come on over here."

During Frank's second week in the hospital, I began to hope a little—not that the damaged part of his lungs would heal but that, with drugs and oxygen and lung therapy, the healthy portions could do the job—and go on doing it for some time.

Frank responded well to treatment. Toward the end of the first week, the infection cleared up. The level of oxygen in his blood rose. One day he walked down the hall and the next day, helped by a nurse, he started climbing stairs.

By the second week, he began rewriting articles for *Defenders* magazine and holding editorial conferences on the phone. His hospital room began to look like his office, with stacks of paper everywhere that no one was allowed to move. When he learned that one of the lung therapists was a lover of wildlife, especially wolves, he asked his associate editor to bring a copy of the issue that carried the wolf poster. "While you're at it, Ken," he said, "bring over enough copies to put in all the waiting rooms. It'll give the place some class."

Eventually the prednisone came down to acceptable levels and all the tubes came out. I took some lessons in lung therapy to help keep his lungs clear, and he came home, a pulmonary invalid at 49.

Chapter 2
Come Live with Me

Come live with me, and be my love
And we will all the pleasures prove
Christopher Marlowe, *The Passionate Shepherd to His Love*

It helped to remember that Frank had a strong will to live and that at least once before in his life he had faced a serious illness and recovered. The illness then had been alcoholism. Two years earlier he had been in a rehabilitation center for alcoholics, his life "thoroughly hashed," as he put it. A superb writer with style and wit, he had found early success, first as a reporter on the Washington *Star* newspaper and then as a writer and photographer on the *National Geographic*. "I thought of myself as the typical newspaperman," he told me, "hard-fighting, hard-loving, hard-drinking."

"I drank my way all the way up the ladder and all the way down," Frank once said. By the time he was 42, he had lost his wife, his home, his job, all his worldly possessions, and many of his friends.

When I met him, he had, against the odds, put his life back together. With the help of Alcoholics Anonymous, he had been sober for more than a year; and to the end of his life, he never drank again. He had won again the love and respect of his two sons, Cris and Adam; and he was getting work as a free-lance writer. In fact, that was how we met.

I had recently been assigned to start a new magazine for the Occupational Safety and Health Administration, a branch of the U.S.

Department of Labor. My qualifications for this job were not readily apparent, even to me. I had never worked on a magazine and knew nothing about safety or health issues. I had been working in the Labor Department's Women's Bureau, where I had made something of a mark as a good speech writer. But the Occupational Safety and Health Act had just been passed, employers all over the country were clamoring for information, and the new agency needed someone fast. I was there; and before I knew it, I was editor-in-chief of a brand-new monthly magazine. I put in three months of 70-hour weeks to learn the craft of magazine editing, and the first couple of issues had marks of the amateur all over them. But I loved the work. I found the whole process exciting—from assigning and editing the articles to laying out pages with graphic designers, to watching the typesetters on the ancient linotype machines the department used then. I felt that I had found my niche as a magazine editor and that one day I would be very good at it.

But I needed help and was desperately looking for free-lance writers who could make technical subjects clear to the lay reader. A phone call to a friend at the National Science Foundation netted two names. Frank Sartwell was one. I phoned. He said he'd be glad to do some free-lance work for the Department of Labor, and we agreed to meet in the office the next day and go out to lunch.

I liked him right away. He had a charming Celtic face and a ready grin. He looked, I thought, a little weather-beaten, in an appealing sort of way, but was really quite good-looking, with his nice, regular features, intense blue eyes, and thick brown hair. He was wearing the right uniform for the business world—white shirt and dark blue suit—but the suit was somewhat shiny, and the cut was a little dated.

It took me no time to realize that he had one of the quickest minds and sharpest wits I had ever encountered and that he had superb qualifications as a writer and editor. I wondered what had happened that such a man was happy to come to my office and discuss free-lance assignments.

Come Live with Me

I figured it out fairly soon. I suggested we go to the Golden Ox for lunch and asked if he knew the place. He did, indeed. He steered us straight into the bar and lounge, which I never knew was there, and the bartender and waiters greeted him by name. I ordered a martini. He ordered a ginger ale. Putting the pieces together, I guessed that he was an alcoholic who had stopped drinking and was making a comeback by doing free-lance work.

He was delightful company. We talked of books and plays and poetry. We discovered that both of us had read Loren Eisley's *Immense Journey* four times and that we liked poetry with structure—like Edna St. Vincent Millay's sonnets. I started to quote a line from a poem by Henry Reed, and Frank finished the line for me. We discussed the Bolshoi Ballet and the possibilities that the Redskins might make the Super Bowl again. We talked of marriages and divorces and whether to bring up the subject of haircuts with teen-age sons.

I liked being with him. What attracted me was that he was so intelligent but also so ready to laugh and have fun. When I talked, he listened intently, his blue eyes looking directly into mine. I got the feeling that he had experienced a lot of things I had only read about, but at the same time he had gentle ways and almost courtly manners. He asked me what I wanted for lunch and then ordered it for me. I never knew anyone who did that, and I liked it.

I found myself wondering how old he was and began asking casual questions about where he had worked and for how long, mentally adding the years together, plus 22 for the age at which he must have graduated from college. Frank observed this for a while and then asked with an amused smile, "Wouldn't it be simpler just to chop me down and count the rings? I'm 44."

"So am I," I responded with a laugh. He said it was clear that some really nice people had been born in 1928, and we looked at each other and smiled.

Half-way through lunch, I finished my martini and declared it a disappointment. "They just don't make a good martini for a woman,"

I said. A strong supporter of women's rights, I could sometimes find discrimination where none existed. "They think women don't know the difference, so they give us weaker ones." Frank gave me an incredulous look and said he doubted that the bartender was back there concocting male and female martinis, but he ordered another for me, anyway.

I found a way to handle the great gulf in our knowledge of magazine editing by simply acknowledging it. I explained that I had been more or less thrown into the job a few months earlier. "I didn't know a pica from a repro when I started," I said, "and I still have an awful lot to learn."

"Well, you're already ahead of the game," Frank said, "because, as long as you don't pretend to know something, you can always learn it."

We talked, finally, of occupational safety and health and of possible free-lance assignments. I wondered if he would find the subject dull. "No," he said. "There are no dull subjects. There are dull writers and dull articles—but dull subjects, no."

Mid-way through my second martini, I began to realize that there hadn't been anything wrong with the first one, after all. I put it down and said, with some embarrassment, that I guessed I didn't have much capacity for liquor. Frank said that was something to be glad, not embarrassed, about.

In the light-headedness brought on not just by the martinis but by something strange and wonderful that the presence of this man did to me, I listed five subjects that would make good articles for the magazine and offered to write him a contract for all five.

"Don't you even want to see how I write first?"

"No. You were highly recommended. I know you're good."

Frank refused to take advantage. "Write a contract for one article. If you like it, write a contract for four more."

The article was great, and a contract for four more followed. For the next year and a half, Frank was the chief free-lance writer for the magazine.

We found lots of reasons to phone each other and to get together. Frank would deliver an article to the office and linger to talk. On a surprising number of days, he would find himself "in the neighborhood" and would come to my office with two huge styrofoam cups of coffee. We would talk and smoke cigarettes for as long as we could reasonably pretend to each other and to ourselves that we were holding an editorial discussion. We both agreed that smoking was a bad habit that we would kick one day. I hoped he could do it; he had a very bad smoker's cough.

Once Frank came by with his two sons, Adam, 13, and Cris, 15. As I looked at their faded blue jeans, old army shirts, and long hair, I found myself relieved to think that Frank already knew what teen-age boys looked like, so that when and if he met my 16-year-old, guitar-playing son Dan, it would not come as a shock.

Whenever Frank traveled anywhere, he sent me notes and postcards, often with some delightfully absurd message. One April, when he went to Charlotte, North Carolina, for a vacation, he sent me a postcard with a huge bank of geraniums on the front and on the back this message:

> I have found 552 safety violations in the flower factories
> here and am staying on to write a series of articles for
> you. Rush check.—Frank

The fact was—and I finally admitted it to myself—that I adored him. After 18 months, I was hopelessly in love. I quoted him like an oracle on every subject. When he came to the office, I sometimes made coffee, and I would get so engrossed in what he was saying that it would flow over the top of the mug and down the credenza. When he left, my concentration was shattered for hours.

In my journal, where I wrote when I needed to "think on paper," I tried to talk myself into a more reasonable state of mind:

> Come on, M, get a grip. Stop acting like an adolescent
> in a first love affair, and remember that you are a mature,
> professional woman with a responsible job. You got out
> of a lousy marriage only two years ago. What's the rush?

A nice pep talk, but my feelings remained as strong as ever. I realized finally that, despite my reluctance to be the first to speak out, I needed to tell Frank how I felt. One day I told him that I needed to talk with him and asked if we could have dinner together. The next day, September 26, we went to the National Press Club, where we had one of our usual animated discussions; but by the time dessert came I still had not found the right opening or the right words. Realizing that I'd better plunge in somehow and soon, I grabbed the first idea that came my way to declare my love: I told Frank he was interfering with my work. He looked up, puzzled. I said I loved being with him, but when he left, I could not concentrate for hours. "And so," I concluded, somewhat breathlessly, "I need to see either more or less of you."

For an instant he was speeches. "Oh," he said at last. Then: "Marcia, there are terrible things about me that you don't know."

"I know you're an alcoholic, Frank, if that's it."

His jaw dropped a little. "How did you know that?"

"I've known it since we first met."

"But you don't know what it means. You don't know where I've been or what I've done."

"Then tell me."

He talked for an hour. He told me about life at the Rehabilitation Center for Alcoholics in Lorton, Virginia, about the jobs he'd lost, about the people he'd let down. He told me what it's like to be without a penny ("The worst thing is you have nothing to give anyone") and how he'd had convulsions from withdrawal three times—once during a job interview ("You wake up in an ambulance with a mouthful of splintered lead pencils"). He told me how hard he'd fought the AA program and how long it took him to get it through his "thick Irish head" that he couldn't drink anymore. He hadn't had a drink for two years, he said, but he couldn't guarantee that he would never drink again. Finally he stopped. He wondered if I wanted to ask him any questions.

"Yes," I said. "When are you going to tell me those terrible things about yourself?"

He stared at me in amazement. Then he smiled and took my hand, and we left the restaurant.

"You got us this far. I'll steer from here," Frank said as we parted that night. We should go "half-speed ahead," which he said was "a course for sensible adults." We would get to know each other slowly; we would make no hasty decisions; we would not talk about marriage for at least two years.

That was September 26, and a whole glorious autumn lay before us. Frank wanted me to know the part of him that loved nature. On weekends we often walked the trails in Rock Creek Park or along the C & O canal, or we headed for Great Falls along the Potomac River. We had a favorite rock overlooking the falls, where we liked to picnic.

I took this photograph of Frank on our favorite rock.

I had always enjoyed nature; now Frank taught me how to really observe it. "Look at the geese heading south for the winter," he said, pointing to some specks in the sky.

"How do you know they're geese?"

"From their silhouettes. See how their wings are set further back than other birds' wings. Look at the length of their necks. Watch how they fly—birds glide sometimes, but geese and ducks have to keep working at it. Their bodies are heavier."

I bought a copy of Roger Tory Peterson's *Birds of North America* and a pair of binoculars, and to Frank's immense delight, eventually got better than he at identifying birds in flight.

Our walks in the woods were usually short. Frank tired before I did, so we would sit down and try to identify birds from their calls. Or we'd talk. Once, when Frank was lying on his back in the woods, his arms outstretched, a gold leaf fluttered down into his hand. "It's a gift from the gods," he said.

On week days when the weather was fine, we met in Lafayette Square or one of Washington's parks and ate lunch together. Lunch hours stretched out. Parting became ridiculously painful. One day when I'd taken a two-and-a-half hour lunch break and positively had to get back to the office, I walked away and, halfway through the park, turned to take one more look at Frank. He was still standing in the same place, watching me. Our eyes met, and we laughed.

We had long ago worked out my role in his alcoholism: I didn't have one. "There is nothing you can do to stop me from drinking if I want to," he said, "and nothing you can do to persuade me to drink if I choose not to. It's my problem. Period."

I wondered if it bothered him when I had a drink.

"No. There is no reason why someone who drinks as moderately as you do shouldn't drink. It only bothers me when someone who really wants a drink orders ginger ale because I'm there. It's as if they think I can't handle the problem without their help. It's annoying."

Come Live with Me

By November Frank thought I should know a little about Alcoholics Anonymous, so he decided to take me to a meeting. At the last minute he had qualms about it. "Suppose you have a terrible reaction to all this?" I said I didn't think it was likely because I knew AA had helped him so much.

The meeting was in a church basement. I had dropped out of church long ago, back when I was in college, feeling that what I heard there was neither true nor relevant. Being back in a church felt strange at first. As the room filled up with eagerly chatting people, though, it didn't seem much like church. The people were a lot more cheerful than I thought they'd be, considering that none of them could ever drink safely again, and they were far from the derelicts I more or less expected. In fact, it was a real cross section of ages and types and looked like a meeting of any club.

Two speakers told their stories about their struggle with alcohol. I was amazed at their honesty and willingness to reveal so much of themselves to a crowd of strangers. I was also surprised at how often the speakers laughed at themselves as they related stories of things they had done or lived through that must have been pretty painful at the time. I admired that, and I thought the laughter must be healing. One speaker gave God a lot of the credit for his sobriety. It stirred old memories of the testimonials I heard as a child in the small-town Methodist church I had attended, and it made me vaguely uncomfortable.

I could understand why Frank at first had resisted the program. There was something wholesome about it that I rather disliked. But AA had given Frank the key to sobriety, and that was the foundation on which he had rebuilt his life. What was good for Frank, I decided, was good. I put Alcoholics Anonymous on the list of things I approved of, and that was that.

By December it was clear that Frank's plan—"half-speed ahead"—was not working. It was agony being apart. We only spent the time figuring out how soon we could be together again. Dating seemed ridiculous—something for teen-agers. After my divorce from the scholarly English professor, I had kept the house in University Park, near the University of Maryland, and occasionally Frank stayed overnight on weekends. We talked about his moving in permanently, but all of this was happening much faster than either of us expected or wanted it to. I took out my journal and debated some issues with myself:

Q. You're doing fine on your own—holding down a good job and raising a fine son. Do you really want to leave your safe harbor and sail into deeper waters?
A. I'm already in them.

Q. Do you love Frank enough to live with him?
A. I really think so.

Q. Besides his intelligence and sense of humor, what qualities do you love him for?
A. His strength—the way he hit bottom and fought his way back, without bitterness or self-pity, and still retaining sweetness and humor and dignity. And his empathy—the way he really listens to what people say. I like it, too, that he doesn't seem to be driven by society's idea of success. He has his own idea of what a successful life is. And his sensitivity; his feelings go deep.

Q. What do you worry about most?
A. He's an unemployed alcoholic—which ought to worry me, but doesn't.

Q. What will people think?
A. My friends will think it's wonderful. Some neighbors may be scandalized. So what?

Q. Will this hurt Dan?
A. Good question. Dan doesn't want to hear bickering in the house again, so this has to work. He hasn't had to share my attention for ages, and maybe that would be a good thing. Also, Frank is a good role model—masculine in a way Dan understands and respects. The important thing is that Dan not feel pushed out.

Q. Will it be awkward for Dan if you and Frank live together?
A. Maybe. But I've never been a conventional mother, and he has never been a conventional kid.

Q. What if Frank has a serious lung problem that gets steadily worse, and all your plans for a fuller, richer life come down to worrying constantly about his health?

I sat there for a full ten minutes searching for an answer. Then I put the pen down, pulled on a coat, and went into the back yard. The air was clear and cold; dusk was falling, but a little wintry light glowed on the horizon. I always loved the yard, but I never realized how magnificent the two big oak trees were, with their branches darkly etched against the setting sun. Some cardinals searched for seeds in the back where it was weedy. Near the steps, where I had thrown some sunflower seeds, a chickadee and a titmouse pecked away contentedly. Before Frank, I had never known how close they would come if you just sat still.

Before Frank: That seemed an eon ago. I thought back on my years with the English professor and about the tedium of that marriage. Now it was replaced by real companionship, and passion, and joy. I was not an ice maiden, after all. For the first time, I knew what it was like to be loved.

I went back in the house and accepted my destiny.

A. Then, somehow, I'll manage.

We decided that Frank would move in after Christmas. "I'll do it slowly," he explained. "We won't hurry this. Maybe I'll just bring a pair of socks or some handkerchiefs every time I come over."
On January 4 Frank packed all his things in a trunk. Friends helped him put it in a station wagon, and he drove home.

CHAPTER 3
Earth Can Be So Sweet

What is the need of Heaven
When earth can be so sweet?
Edna St. Vincent Millay, *Interim*

How could I have overlooked the innate conservatism of children—especially when judging a parent's behavior? It wasn't my neighbors who were scandalized by the new living arrangements. It was my own son, Dan, the long-haired, hip, aspiring rock guitarist.

"At your age you're supposed to be through with such stuff!" he told me.

"What do you mean 'at my age'? I'm 46!"

"*That's* what I mean!"

Dan remained aloof for nearly six months. Then he softened. "I realize you have the same rights as anyone else," he said. I suspect, though, that he just began to enjoy Frank's company too much to hold out any longer. They had begun a kind of verbal ping-pong match at meals to see who could top the other's best line. It's hard to stay aloof when the opposition is roaring with laughter at one of your jokes. Dan's affection for Frank, when it came, was whole-hearted and unwavering.

Frank and I were, quite simply, gloriously happy together. Nothing had ever prepared me for the fact that life could be so much fun—certainly not my childhood, for I had arrived in that small Pennsylvania town at a time when my parents neither wanted nor could afford a second child; nor my 15-year marriage to the English professor for whom the house always had to be quiet so that he could "write"—an activity that seldom actually took place because "writer's block" prevented it. Frank wrote not only beautifully, but easily—sometimes at the kitchen table, in the midst of noise and activity. He worked hard, but he also knew how to play. He played with ideas, with words, with plans and dreams. He saw possibilities in almost everything. There was an endless list of things he wanted to do, read about, write about, or photograph. And to him, all of these pleasures were better if he shared them. He often invited me into a new venture with lines from Frost's "The Pasture":

>   I'm going out to clean the pasture spring;
>   I'll only stop to rake the leaves away
>   (And wait to watch the water clear, I may)
>   I sha'n't be gone long.—You come too.

He could put fun into almost any activity. One January day shortly after he moved in, Frank was working on a free-lance job not far from where I worked. As we drove into town together, light snow was falling. By mid-afternoon it looked like a blizzard. At 3 o'clock all government employees were dismissed. I called Frank and arranged to pick him up in ten minutes. When I drove to his building, though, he wasn't there. Five minutes went by. I began to get anxious. Didn't he know that snow could make driving in the Washington traffic a nightmare? Suddenly he emerged from a nearby restaurant smiling and carrying a paper bag. Settling into the car, he produced two steaming cups of coffee and a bag of brownies. "If we have to drive home in a blizzard," he said, "we might as well make a party of it."

A light snowfall created the opportunity for Frank to stomp out a 30-foot valentine.

We seemed awfully well suited to each other. We had only one issue that caused friction with any frequency—and that was our children. We were both trying too hard to atone for the past.

When Frank had hit bottom, Cris was 11, and Adam 9. While Frank struggled with his alcoholism, there was a period of almost a year when he did not see his sons. It must have felt like abandonment to them. Frank once said, "If I could have gotten sober for Cris and Adam, I would have done it. You cannot get sober for someone else, no matter how much you love them. You have to get sober for yourself." Now that Frank had his life together again, he wanted to make everything up to them. In the meantime, Frank's ex-wife, who still lived in the Chevy Chase home on the other side of town, had married a respected high school teacher. Cris and Adam, I thought, were all right now. They did not need Frank as much as he needed them. They loved him, and they did want to be with him—just not as often as he wanted it.

I wanted as much time as I could have with Frank, and I often resented the amount of time he spent with his sons. Frank felt the same way about me. He thought I gave Dan too much time and attention. Some lingering guilt about the divorce, he suspected, made me too indulgent and too quick to buy him everything he wanted.

We were both right. In time, we got better at dealing with our feelings, but they were always there to some extent, the only discordant note in our partnership.

In June Frank was offered a job as editor of a magazine published by the Atomic Industrial Forum. It was highly technical. He would have to cram a lot of nuclear physics into his head in a short time.

"Can you *do* that?"

"Yes."

"I didn't think you took any science in college."

"I didn't. A good thing, too. Anything I learned then would be wrong by now."

He decided to finish his free-lance assignments and take a brief vacation before starting the new job. I took it upon myself to plan a five-day vacation at the ocean. A friend told me of the wonderful time she and her husband had at an old hotel in a fishing resort called Wachapreague on the coast of Virginia. It sounded enchanting, and I made reservations.

A couple of weeks later, when we arrived there, my heart fell. It was an old hotel, all right. Almost decrepit, in fact. There was no beach. The only other guests were fishermen, who sloshed through the lobby wearing enormous rubber boots and carrying buckets of flounder. Then I remembered: My friend loved to fish. I didn't. Frank didn't, either. I had made a terrible mistake. By the time we got to our room (lumpy bed, just as I feared), I felt guilty and was thoroughly berating myself. We had so little time for vacations, and I had ruined it by coming here.

"Marcia," Frank said. "You can have fun anywhere you are."

Earth Can Be So Sweet

I doubted it, but I was about to learn from an expert. Early the next morning, Frank rented a boat, bought a navigational map, and steered us six miles out to sea to Cedar Island, one of the barrier islands off the coast of Virginia. We had the whole island to ourselves except for the shore birds. A lot of willets were nesting there. We had to be careful not to walk too close, for whenever we did, they would squawk furiously and dive at us. We would retreat, laughing and snapping photos of the birds, their beaks open to scold, the V-shaped black and white markings of their wings bold against the blue sky. We spent a wonderful afternoon swimming, picnicking, walking the beach, and watching birds. Then when we realized it was getting late and a storm seemed to be brewing, we discovered that the boat wouldn't start.

We understood then why the man who rented it to us had shouted, "Good luck," as we pushed off. We were marooned! Half an hour later, when being marooned was getting too cold and scary to be fun anymore, a Coast Guard boat came within hailing distance. It towed us back through choppy waters and darkening skies to the mainland.

We arrived at the hotel drenched from the waves that had washed over the boat, chilled to the bone, ravenously hungry, and dead tired. The home-cooked food at the hotel was delicious, the bed was not so lumpy as to keep anyone awake, and neither of us minded if friendly fishermen came and went at odd hours carrying gear and buckets of fish.

After that, a spirit of high adventure prevailed, and we spent four glorious days exploring the nearby marshes, beaches, and towns.

Frank's ability to accept whatever situation he was in, to live each moment, to find fun—and, if possible, share it—was a quality he had won the hard way. He had been on the bottom rung of society and had wrested this capacity for joy from despair, poverty, and humiliation. It touched the lives of people who knew him; and slowly it began to change me, to make me realize that life could be more than work and duty and a feeling of martyrdom. "You have an enormous capacity to enjoy life," Frank once told me. "Let it grow."

With his help it did. It even met the acid test of Christmas, a season that I usually struggled through in a thinly disguised Nordic melancholy. As that season approached, I prepared to meet it with my usual heroic determination to make it nice for everyone and not to let anyone see how much I disliked it all.

Frank would have none of this. First of all, he said, I was starting too soon. No one was allowed to think about Christmas until after his birthday—November 28. Christmas was fine in its place, he said, but its place was after his birthday. Also, we were instructed not to hold back on buying him birthday presents simply because there would soon be another opportunity to buy him more presents.

On November 29, though, the lid was off. Frank was making a good salary. What was money for if not to buy presents? We had three wonderful sons. Weren't we lucky, he said, that they were all past the age when they wanted plastic toys? Now we could buy them interesting things. Didn't I agree that a sweater of black sheep's wool would make a great gift for Cris? "He'd love the poetry of that, I think," Frank said. Dan could use a set of tools for repairing guitars. Now, how about Adam? We poured over catalogues and ads. It *was* fun! "What the hell," I thought, "I might as well take some time off work and go all out."

Packages began to pile up under the Christmas tree. Frank's joy in buying presents was contagious. He picked out wonderful things—tools, books, games that would open new avenues for the one receiving them. From the fireplace mantel we hung stockings that quickly overflowed, requiring additional containers labeled "auxiliary stockings."

All the boys were with us on Christmas Day. They seemed to enjoy getting together. Cris and Adam even agreed, just for the day, to stop pummeling each other on the slightest provocation. However trying they might be at times, they were surely a bunch of talented kids: Dan was a dedicated musician; Cris had clearly inherited the Sartwell writing ability and was concentrating on poetry; Adam, the youngest, was probably also the brightest and most versatile; he was adept at science and math, yet equally interested in literature, art, and music. Dan was the only one who played an instrument, but they all loved music, especially rock and jazz. At Christmas, they exchanged records, vying with each other to find and give a dynamite record no one else had yet discovered. So music filled the air at our house on Christmas, though not exactly the traditional kind.

Among the gifts were hiking gear and poetry books for Cris, guitar accessories (fuzz pedal and wah-wah pedals among them) for Dan, scientific and mathematical gadgets for Adam, binoculars for Frank, a camera for me. Afterwards we sat down to a great Christmas dinner. I did not like the everyday routine of cooking, but I did enjoy preparing a dinner for special occasions. I went all out: scalloped oysters, a perfectly roasted turkey, mashed potatoes, sweet potatoes, two kinds of cranberry sauce, an array of vegetables. My secret weapon, though, was that somewhere along the line I had learned the art of making a terrific pie crust. I kept this art a secret for the most part, but on this occasion, I presented two triumphant pies, mincemeat and pumpkin. Afterwards, Dan played some traditional Christmas carols on the guitar, resisting, for the most part, the urge to make them rock.

Frank's happiness was complete. He had his sons with him; he had a home that he could bring them to. He had a good job. Five years earlier, his troubles were compounded by the fact that he had "nothing to give anyone." Now he had enough to give generously.

After his boys had gone home and Dan had left to jam with some local musicians, Frank and I sat in front of the fire, literally amid the wrappings of Christmas. "You have made it possible for me to live as I would have been living if there had been no alcoholic crash," Frank said. "I have my sons back. I have my life back. I have you. And you are inexpressibly dear to me."

In February Frank was offered another job—as editor of *Defenders*, a magazine published by Defenders of Wildlife. Natural history was his first love. "It's like coming home," he said.

I changed jobs, too, and went to work for the National Endowment for the Arts as the director of publications. Now we both worked in the fields that mattered most to us. We were a couple of awfully lucky people, we thought.

In September Dan took his guitar and went off to the Berklee College of Music in Boston, and Chris enrolled in the University of Maryland. The boys were growing up, and we were coming to the end of our first two years together. One day, in the midst of a particularly good roast beef dinner, Frank proposed. When Dan came home for Thanksgiving, Frank formally asked him for my hand in marriage.

Dan was a little flustered. "Gosh, I thought you two. . .Well, yes. *Sure*. That's great!"

We decided to get married during Christmas vacation. The first day of the new year seemed just right. "The bells will always ring on the eve of our anniversary," Frank said, "and we will know they ring for us."

Married life was even better. Everything deepened—our joy in being together, our understanding of each other, our quiet contentment.

Frank felt ready to tackle his smoking problem. He had been reluctant to give it up before; however harmful the habit was, he thought it might help relieve tension that could lead to drinking. Now he thought he could give up smoking, too. I decided to quit along with him.

We enrolled in Smokenders, a group program that helped us cut down over a period of five weeks. At the end of that time, we tossed our cigarettes away.

We spent our first cigarette-less day in Chincoteague, Virginia, scrubbing the walls of an old farmhouse Frank had bought. Our theory was that being up to your elbows in soapy water all day makes it very difficult to smoke, and that if we did not smoke that first day, we had the problem licked. The theory was correct; neither of us ever smoked again.

Earth Can Be So Sweet

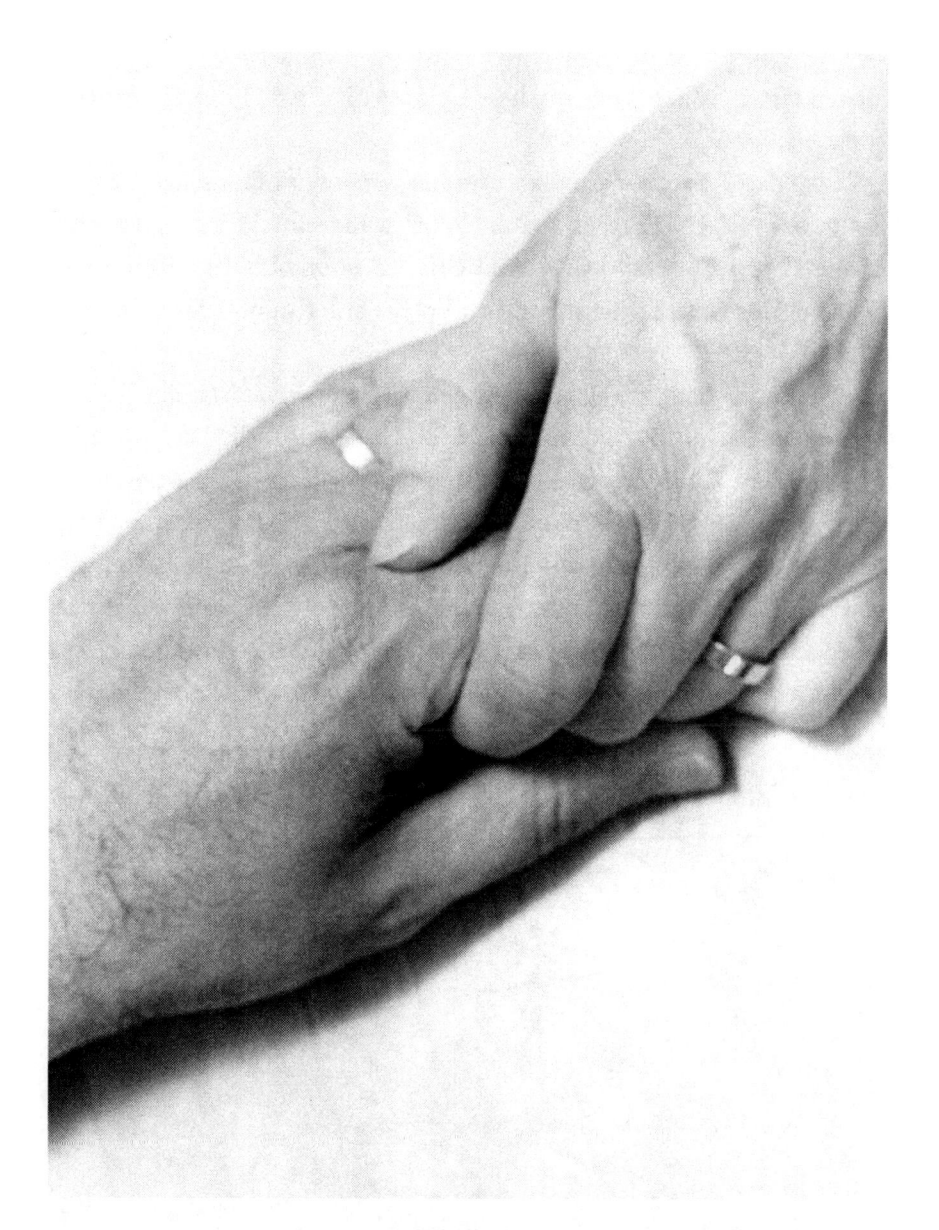

Frank took this photograph with his free hand

Frank's health improved dramatically. The terrible cough that used to halt conversations in restaurants went away. He looked better and moved faster. When I put my head against his chest, I didn't hear that wheeze anymore.

One day I watched from an upstairs window as Frank and Cris set out to have lunch together. Frank looked wonderful. "I feel better than I have in years," he told Cris. And Cris, 18 years old but still with all his emotions close to the surface, threw his arms around his father and cried.

Frank had bought the farmhouse on Chincoteague Island, Virginia, because he had always wanted a place on that part of the Eastern shore. The town of Chincoteague is a fisherman's village where clamming ships dominate the harbor and oystermen work their trade among the salt marshes. A bridge links Chincoteague with Assateague Island, site of a wildlife refuge that is famous for its long-legged wading birds—especially herons and egrets—its snow geese, and its wild ponies. The spot is a natural for a lover of birds and editor of a wildlife magazine.

These binoculars were my first Christmas gift to Frank

Frank loved the dunes, marshes, woodlands, and quiet beaches. He loved watching flights of snow geese arriving in October; seeing a sandpiper snatch a morsel from the sea and scamper away inches ahead of a breaking wave; finding that one of the "gulls" circling overhead was actually an osprey, an endangered species of hawk now making a comeback. He loved the marsh grass, which changed color with every season and in the fall was etched in white by a row of pearl-like seeds along the side. For Frank, owning a place on the island was the fulfillment of a dream. When he closed the deal on the farmhouse, he wrote me a card:

> After signing the papers, I went out to look at the place. As I came out of the house, an American egret flew overhead and flapped its great wings like a benediction.

I came to love Chincoteague, too; that is, I loved everything about it except the farmhouse. It had no view of water, for one thing. Worse, it reminded me of my childhood during the Depression, when some of my poorer relatives had lived in houses like that. To me, it just wasn't a beach house. It brought back memories of hard times and cold winters, and I could not erase the association. Frank was disappointed but it couldn't be helped: I never really liked the place.

One day in late March we took a walk along the waterfront in Chincoteague. The marsh grass was burnished gold against the blue sky, the air was crisp and clear, and Frank was setting a pace he never could have maintained when he was smoking. We both were exhilarated; so much seemed possible now, so much seemed to lie ahead for us.

We came across a lot for sale, an ideal spot for a cottage. Situated on a small inlet on Chincoteague Bay, the property faced the bay side of Assateague Island. It commanded a breath-taking view; and we discovered, by climbing a ladder someone had left leaning against a nearby cottage, that every rung up improved it. From fifteen feet up, you could see miles in either direction, a spectacular vista of water, marshes, woods, and lighthouse.

We never tired of this view because it was never the same.

We guessed that the price might be around $5,000. If we could get it for that, we would buy it. We didn't have to build on it. We could just own it. Come over for picnics. Have it for an investment.

The price was $20,000—in cash, no mortgages. We thanked the agent for the information and went back to the farmhouse. Outrageous. Who had that kind of money? In cash? Out of the question.

Gloom hung over dinner that night. And over the evening, and over most of breakfast next morning.

"Wait a minute," I said. "I could put a second mortgage on the house and get the cash that way."

"A cottage built on that spot would really rent," Frank said.

"We could rent it in the summer and have it for ourselves the rest of the year."

"And if it were a business property, there would be deductions for depreciation, and for interest. . ."

"We can retire there and you can write great books about Chincoteague."

"We can eat oysters and clams every day. We could dig for them ourselves."

We were racing each other for the car.

We offered $18,000. "Would he take that, do you think?" we asked the agent.

He would. I put a second mortgage on my house, arranged new financing, and we bought the land, putting it in both our names. When we got the deed, I frowned a little; then we both chuckled: "Property of Frank Sartwell *et ux.*" The lawyer said he didn't see what was funny, and Frank said something to the effect that it "depends on whose *ux* is gored."

Frank sold the farmhouse and arranged to finance the building of the cottage. We drew plans for a house with two bedrooms and a porch on the first floor, and the living room, dining area, and kitchen on the second floor to make the most of the view. The front of the house would face the water and would be floor-to-ceiling glass. We would leave as many trees as possible so that the house would be hidden among them. We would leave the terrain rough, with its little sand dunes; and we would leave the wild raspberry bushes and thistles so that the birds would come. "They won't even know we're here," Frank said.

Frank bought me a camera and critiqued my pictures, so that every once in a while I could get off a good shot.

We turned the plans over to an architect who could translate them into reality and hoped to move in by October in time to see the snow geese arrive.

Dear Richard:

Here is the $1,000 retainer on your services as designer and construction superintendent on the house on Piney Island in Chincoteague. It's a day late, perhaps, but I had a little trouble remembering where I buried the jar. Marcia and I are delighted you'll be putting your creativity into the project, and, of course, we're getting more excited as we realize what we're up to. We are convinced that there should be some space available as a "writing room" or something very much like one. If I do in fact write the world's greatest book about Chincoteague by a left-handed tight end of Irish extraction, it'll help to have a place to sit while doing it.

Be of good cheer.

Frank

The construction of the house met with every possible delay. By October only the pilings were in. By December there was only the shape of a house outlined in 2 x 4's. We spent a melancholy hour or two there one grey December afternoon, each of us trying to hide our disappointment from the other. The next year would bring better things, we promised ourselves.

But the next year brought the flu in January and Frank's hospitalization in March.

CHAPTER 4
Master of Fantasy

I am the master of fantasy.
Arthur Rimbaud, *Nuit de L'Enfer*

When Frank came home from the hospital, I sensed—despite his optimism and some carefully phrased doctors' comments that could be construed as hopeful—that this was the beginning of the end. At that time I had no idea what a long ending it would be, what it would be like, or what it would do to me. I did not know that I would do things I never thought I'd do and think in ways that once would have shocked me. I did not know that the long ending would wear down all defenses and all illusions and leave only raw emotion, or that I would have to confront feelings so powerful and so painful that they would shatter my views about what kind of person I was.

Over the three years of Frank's decline, I was a human being under extreme stress, and it brought out the best—and the worst—in me. Though I was happy to find reserves of strength I never knew I had, I was appalled to uncover the depth of my rage and fury. I was equally appalled to discover that there were times when I longed to save my own life at any cost and to smash and destroy things as wantonly as I felt my own life was being destroyed. In the end, all I wanted was to get through it—it didn't matter how.

In the beginning, though, I wanted to be perfect. I wanted to have all the right qualities—selflessness, courage, endless good humor, unfailing strength, "grace under pressure." I wanted to be everything Frank needed. Since I didn't know anyone who had been through a similar experience, and since my efforts to discuss it with people only drew conventional pieties ("Be brave, my dear") or caused them to pull away from me, I took a lot of my ideas from books and movies. I thought our troubles should draw us closer as we faced them together. I had some notions, gathered, I guess, from *Readers' Digest* articles, that, when life was suddenly cut short, people found a way to live each day so fully that they crammed a lifetime of joy into the time they had left. That was what I thought we should do.

So I tried to set my feelings aside—tried to ignore the shock I still felt at the lightning speed with which our lives had changed, tried to suppress my grief and self-pity at the prospect of losing him. Such emotions seemed wrong and selfish at such a time. I was determined to hide them from Frank and even from myself.

I also wanted to overcome my fear of illness. All my life I had fled it, excusing myself on the grounds that I just was not good with sick people. One of my fervent hopes had always been that I would never have to face a long illness—my own or anybody else's. Now life had handed me the wrong problem, one I was singularly ill-equipped to deal with. For Frank I thought I could change, though; I would have to. I recalled how he once condemned a relative who had walked out on a sick husband: "We Sartwells do not abandon our wounded." She had broken a code. I must never do that. Whatever lay ahead, I had to hold up under it. We would face our troubles together, and I would do "the right thing."

Frank's approach to his illness, though, made figuring out "the right thing" a more daunting task than I thought it would be. For while I denied my feelings, he denied the facts. I got a foretaste of the difficulties to come when he insisted, on one of his first days home, that a proposed move of his editorial offices be carried out. This meant moving his office from the first floor to the third floor of a walk-up building. Nobody wanted to do it, but nobody wanted to spell out the reasons.

"Why do it?" I asked. "You're fine as you are."

"I am not fine. The staff is scattered all over the building. It's a much better space for putting out a magazine, and I had to fight to get it."

"It's an awful lot of stairs."

"I can climb stairs now. In six months I'll be able to climb them just that much better."

The move was carried out, and for the rest of his life, Frank had to cope with two long flights of stairs to his office. I always felt that I had let him down by not somehow blocking the move, but I would also have let him down if I had not supported his optimism and determination to live as fully as he could.

As for facing our troubles together, it soon became clear that we did not agree on what we were facing. Frank clung to the belief that he was going to get well—at least as well as he was before he caught the flu. I thought the flu had done extensive lung damage and that his two weeks in the hospital had brought him back about as far as he could come. I hoped he could stay there for a long time and not lose ground.

We even interpreted the same information differently. Shortly after leaving the hospital, Frank tape-recorded a talk with one of the doctors. What Frank heard ("I'd say the prognosis is quite good") confirmed his belief that he would get well. Listening to the same tape, I heard evasions and qualifications everywhere. When Frank asked, "Doctor, if the prognosis is good, why am I not getting better faster?" I heard the embarrassment in the doctor's voice as he explained that "good is a relative term."

Yet there were times when I allowed myself to hope that Frank was right—that he would get better, that we had a long married life ahead of us. I knew the facts did not point that way: that the lungs, once damaged, do not heal, that there was no cure for emphysema. But the opposite seemed equally unbelievable—that after one brief year of marriage my husband was dying. It didn't seem possible that such a thing had happened to me. Those things happened in books, in movies, maybe to other people. And it had happened so suddenly. Maybe, I thought, it will stop just as suddenly, and I will see how needlessly worried I have been.

Then, too, in the beginning Frank's determination was so strong and his spirits so buoyant that he sometimes convinced me that the rules didn't apply. For surely if anyone could charm the gods into reversing the fates—or the course of an incurable illness—it would be Frank, with his wit, his exuberance for life, and his cheerful assumption that if he just committed himself to a full life, the means to live it would somehow follow.

He was so outrageously unrealistic that I sometimes thought it just might work. Whenever he could draw a decent breath, ideas and plans for good times would flow, and he would plot daring deeds to defy his illness. It was as if he had decided that if he refused to take the illness seriously, it could not be a serious illness.

He wanted me to go along with it. And often, over-riding my misgivings and concerns, I did. It is his illness, I thought; surely he has a right to choose his own weapons in dealing with it. He has chosen denial. Who am I to say that's wrong?

Sometimes his determination to act as if he were well, or getting there, was wonderful. He would set out to do something no one thought he could do and bring it off. Everyone's spirits would be boosted. More often, though, it created problems—practical ones and emotional ones.

One day shortly after coming home from the hospital, Frank startled me by asking, "How would you like to go on a whaling trip?"

"Whaling trip?"

"Yes. An ad came in the mail this morning. A ship leaves Ocean City at 6 in the morning and goes 60 miles into the Atlantic. They almost always sight whales, which migrate this time of year. But even if you don't see whales, there are lots of sea birds."

I gasped as I studied the ad. It made no attempt to conceal the fact that it was a strenuous 16-hour trip designed for the hardy. The possibilities for disaster flooded in so fast I could scarcely sort them out. Suppose we managed somehow to get on the ship and, 60 miles out at sea in the damp, cold air, Frank began gasping for breath. What would we do if none of the medicines helped? Would they turn the ship around and come back? Would it help if they did? Did we have a right to jeopardize other people's trips? What would people think of me if I took a sick man on a trip like that?

I floundered about trying to find a way to handle the situation. I wanted to protect his morale as well as his health, and I knew that the emphysema patient with a positive attitude does better than one who thinks of himself as an invalid.

"I don't think you're up to it yet," I said finally.

"It's not till next month. I'll be fine by then," he said.

I tried another approach. "We'll have to get up awfully early to get to Ocean City by 6 o'clock."

"We'll go down the night before and stay in a motel."

I gave in. I choose to line up with his reckless plan rather than reveal my lack of faith that his health would improve. It was the only way to stay emotionally close to Frank, and I needed to do that. I would not undermine him or become his opponent. It may not have been the right decision, but already the ground was too slippery to know the right move from the wrong.

For the next month Frank enjoyed planning "the whaling expedition," and I pretended to be as enthusiastic as he about the plans and concealed my fear that we might actually try to carry them out. Then his editorial responsibilities provided a reprieve. At the last minute he announced that he had too much work to do and that we would have to put off the trip until fall, when the whales migrated again.

Thus began what I came to think of as "the game," in which we pretended that Frank would soon be well or, later, that he was not as ill as he really was. At first it was not so awfully difficult to play the game. It created some worries for me, but it seemed to support Frank's determination not to let the situation depress him. As his condition worsened, though, it became more difficult to conceal my anxiety and act out an optimism I did not feel. I began to need a couple of scotches to get the necessary distance from reality to play it.

In time I came to hate the game. When we should have been drawing closer together and helping each other, we were, instead, involved in an elaborate game of denial. Frank had chosen his way of coping with his troubles, and I pretended to go along with it. I kept my dark thoughts to myself and felt increasingly lonely. We did not talk honestly about his dying. Each of us faced it alone.

CHAPTER 5
Tho' Much Is Taken

Tho' much is taken, much abides.
Alfred, Lord Tennyson, *In Memoriam*

Frank and I may not have agreed on what we faced, but we were in absolute agreement that the best way to go forward was to look at what was left and try to hang on to it.

Quite a lot was left. For me, life with Frank, even a somewhat incapacitated Frank, was still infinitely happier than any life I had ever known before, and I wanted all of it that I could have.

We tried every trick we knew and every bit of helpful technology we could find to keep him going. We got rid of his beloved old Volkswagen because shifting gears exhausted him. We bought a car with automatic everything. He hated it; he said terrible things to it; but he drove it. He even swallowed his pride and got a license plate for handicapped persons. "I don't really need it," he grumbled, "but I get better parking places this way."

We put air conditioners and dehumidifiers in every room to cope with Washington's hot and humid summers. Winters, though, were the most dangerous. In cold air his lungs spasmed and shut down completely, and he could not breathe until he got into warm air. It was terrifying for both of us when that happened. To avoid it, I always warmed up the car and parked as close as I could to the front door. Then, his face buried in a scarf, Frank came out, trying not to breathe too deeply but not to hold his breath, either. When we arrived at our destination, I drove him as close to the entrance as I could.

I had always been the kind of person who, if a sign said Do Not Walk on the Grass, would not walk on it. Now, without a qualm, I disregarded signs that said Do Not Enter, Wrong Way, or No Stopping. Nor did I make fine distinctions about whether the "road" I was using was really a road, a sidewalk, or someone's front yard. When Frank wanted to go somewhere, I drove him there.

Frank had the dignity of work for the rest of his life, thanks to the staff and board of Defenders of Wildlife, which valued him as an editor and did everything possible to accommodate his needs. They bought a dehumidifier and heater for his office and had the air conditioner serviced. They also bought a couch in case he should want to lie down, not knowing that he would rather die at his desk than show such weakness.

Frank worked three days in the office and two at home. In the first year, he often drove to the office. After that, I drove and dropped him off on my way to work. Ignoring the traffic jam that I regularly created, I carried his briefcase, lunch, and books into the lobby. A staff member picked them up and took them upstairs. Then Frank started the climb to this third-floor office. The organization would gladly have moved his office downstairs again, but he would have none of it. The climb took about twenty minutes, and on the last leg of it, the sounds of his gasping were awful. Frank pretended it wasn't a struggle. The staff pretended not to notice.

He joined a class given by the hospital for emphysema patients—"How To Breathe Without Lungs," he called it. The class taught him a better way to climb stairs, appropriate exercises ("jog twice around the dining room table"), and a way of breathing through pursed lips that made the most sustained use of the oxygen taken in.

We learned about the effects, and side effects, of various medications. The basic medications were broncho-dilators—pills and sprays that opened up the lung passageways. The basic side effect was that they made him jittery. Then there was prednisone, the drug that made a huge difference in how he felt, but which could also destroy muscle tissue, soften bones by breaking down the marrow, and create edema.

We bought a "breathing machine" known as an IPPB (for intermittent positive pressure breathing). Frank would place a plastic mask over his nose and mouth, and the machine forced warm, medicated air into his lungs. Since he needed to do this every four hours, we began to feel that our lives were tethered to the IPPB.

On the surface, I seemed to be accepting the situation and making the best of it. And eventually it began to seem that illness had always been part of our daily lives. In the beginning, though, the pain of it stabbed anew every day. At night I would have dreams in which Frank was well. Waking, I would feel a terrible sadness that I could not comprehend. What was that heavy feeling in my chest? Why did I feel like crying? Then it would all come back: Frank was ill.

"Keep as active as you can, Frank," advised Dr. Steinberg, a pulmonologist and Frank's new doctor. "Just be careful. Don't catch a cold—and, Marcia, don't you catch one and bring it home to him. Stay out of crowds. If you want to take in a show, don't go to a small theater. Go to a larger, airier place like the Kennedy Center."

It never occurred to me that a person could not catch colds. I always considered two colds each winter part of the human condition. Nevertheless, I set out to avoid them. I took vitamins, stayed out of crowded places, and avoided people with colds. Staff members with colds called me on the telephone or talked to me from the hall outside my office. I developed a remarkable ear for detecting whether anyone nearby had a cough or sniffle. If it was within my power, I sent the offender out of the room. If not, then I moved. Once, during a meeting of the National Council on the Arts, I changed seats five times in one afternoon until I was entirely satisfied with the respiratory condition of everyone with hearing range. I went through three winters without a cold. It was the only thing I did as perfectly as I had intended.

Do Not Go Gentle

We wanted to keep going to plays, concerts, and musicals as long as we could. That required careful planning so that Frank could be on the IPPB every four hours, but we thought it was doable and worth the effort. When "Chorus Line" came to the Kennedy Center, we decided to give it a try. Our timing was impeccable: as soon as Frank finished with the IPPB, we left the house, arriving at the Kennedy Center half an hour later—early enough for me to drive up to the entrance and drop him off. The theater was on the same level; he had only about 20 yards to walk and no stairs. By the time I parked the car in the underground garage, he was already in his seat. No one around us seemed to have a cold. Frank even walked out to the lobby at intermission. We were in good spirits when the show ended, and we still had 45 minutes before Frank needed to be home.

We had forgotten, however, how difficult it would be for me to pick up Frank at the entrance, where a huge knot of people, taxis, and cars was snarled. It seemed better to stay together and get the car, which was parked not far from the escalator. Frank made it all right, and I pulled into the line of cars waiting to exit.

Five minutes later we had moved only inches. The huge garage was bumper-to-bumper with cars, all with their motors running. The air became dense with carbon monoxide fumes.

"We've got to get out of here soon," Frank said tensely.

I turned up the air conditioning, hoping it would filter the air more effectively. The car got colder, but the air didn't improve. My eyes were smarting. What must this be like for Frank?

"I can't take this," he said, leaning forward against the dashboard. His breath was coming noisily, in great gasps.

Despite the air conditioning, perspiration streamed down my face. Should I leave the car and look for help? Could one of the attendants get us out? Where were they, anyway?

Suddenly one of the lines began to move. I saw an opening and nosed a fender in front of a car in the moving lane. "Please!" I shouted through the window. He couldn't have heard me, but he shrugged and waved us in. A few minutes later, when we hit the clean air of Rock Creek Park, Frank breathed more easily, and so did I.

The experience didn't mark the end of our going to concerts and plays, but after that we always approached such events with as much apprehension as pleasure. We learned the obvious lesson, of course: it was better to wait until the crowd thinned out before we left. That had its drawbacks, too, but not such serious ones. Once, as we sat in a theater after a play, the usher approached us.

"Sorry, folks, you can't stay here. We have to clean up for the next performance."

We rose and, arm in arm, took what must have seemed a defiantly slow pace up the aisle.

"Move along, now," he said irritably. "I can't wait all day."

I turned and was about to explain when I realized that Frank was enjoying the situation. The usher could not see that he was ill. He was treating Frank just like anyone else, and Frank loved it.

As time went on, though, the amount of work and anxiety involved in going to the theater generally outweighed the pleasure of it. We made plans and bought tickets because neither of us wanted to admit defeat. Often, though, a day or two before the performance, Frank would say that he had too much work to do or that he had read the reviews and didn't think it was his kind of play—perhaps I should take a friend. I was surprised, though, when he back out of seeing a revival of *Oklahoma!* because that was, indeed, his kind of show.

I took Dan, who was home on spring break, and went to the show, anyway, because Frank always felt worse if he caused me to miss something. It was a great performance, and Frank would have loved it. Somewhere, in one of the funny scenes at the beginning, I thought how heartily he would be laughing if he were with me, and my eyes filled with tears. After that, the funnier the show got, the more I missed

Frank and the more I cried. It was ludicrous and I knew it, but there in the comforting darkness, I let the tears flow.

Dan gave me an incredulous look at first and then understood. Afterwards, driving home, he tried to kid me into a better mood:

"It sure is weird going to a comedy with you, Mom," he said.

But I did not cheer easily that day. I had had a foretaste of what it would be like when Frank's great laugh was stilled forever, and the loneliness of it was awesome.

Chapter 6
A Ceaseless Rain

> Sorrow like a ceaseless rain
> Beats upon my heart
> Edna St. Vincent Millay, *Sorrow*

That summer was a season of losses, large and small. The bitterest was the loss of the Chincoteague dream.

Frank fretted that he wasn't "getting well" as fast as he expected. He decided it was because he hadn't had a real vacation since leaving the hospital. His proposed remedy was Chincoteague, where the builders were finally finishing our cottage. Frank was sure that if he could just spend a couple of weeks there, the clean air, sun, and the closeness to nature would restore him to health.

"It will do you good, too," he said. "Whether you know it or not, you need to get away. That job has made you awfully tense lately."

I was doubtful, but he was almost giddy with anticipation. As we began to plan our vacation there, his excitement carried me along. We wanted to get photographs of shore birds that were good enough for Frank to publish in *Defenders*. To save our energy, we'd set up a blind in the marshes and wait, very still, until the birds came into camera range. That way we could get excellent photographs without walking much. From one spot we could photograph a variety of species: tiny sandpipers and dunlins, oyster catchers, curlews, avocets, black-bellied plovers. Yes! That would work.

From our living room on the second floor we would watch birds against a vast expanse of marsh and water: terns and gulls patrolling the canal in front of the cottage, willets nesting in the marshes on the opposite bank, beyond that, circling over Assateague Bay, more gulls, perhaps an occasional osprey, maybe, with luck, a peregrine falcon. And from any direction we might see egrets, herons, swans, ibises. Oh, it would be glorious!

We would find the most beautiful place on the ocean beach and picnic there. It wouldn't be necessary to walk the beach and change the view. From one spot you could find a world of beauty if you knew how to look—and Frank did.

We just took photographs; we didn't keep things.

We would drive along the five-mile road that looped the refuge. From the car we could watch the famous, not-very-wild Chincoteague ponies, allegedly brought to the island in the seventeenth century when a Spanish galleon sank. More difficult to find, but possible if you knew where to look, were the miniature elk. Perhaps we would see again the otter family whose house in the river bank we had spotted the year before.

We would eat our fill of seafood: fresh Chincoteague oysters, probably the best in the world; crab cakes, clam chowder, flounder stuffed with crab. Fried fish. In the humblest Chincoteague eatery you could get fried fish that the fanciest Washington restaurants could not surpass.

It was impossible not to get caught up in it.

Maybe our dreams had only been interrupted, not destroyed. Maybe the flu had not damaged Frank's health permanently. Maybe he would lie in the sun, and rest, and regain his strength—or at least some of it.

Chincoteague became such an obsession with Frank that he lusted to be there, even if the cottage wasn't yet finished. He called the architect, Richard Vesely, who was keeping an eye on construction, and told him to push things along because we were coming down in two weeks.

We decided that I should go down a day early and get things ready. When the day arrived, I loaded the station wagon with kitchen utensils, bedding, and curtains and started out on the 175-mile trip under grey skies. Half-way there I stopped and pulled a sweater out of the suitcase. It was really cold for June.

"Well, you've got water," Richard said when I pulled into the driveway. Three workmen in muddy boots were filling in a trench that held the water line. The scene was bleak: grey water and grey skies, the yard a churned-up sea of mud.

"Any electricity?"

"Three wall outlets work. The kitchen range isn't hooked up yet; neither are the heating units."

"What about the Franklin stove?"

"It's in, but the stove pipe isn't connected."

We went inside and climbed the flight of stairs to the second floor, which was living room, dining room, and kitchen combined. Through the floor-to-ceiling glass doors that made up the entire front of the house, I got a splendid 180 degree panorama of fog.

"Where did the view go?"

"Sorry about that. It was beautiful here last week."

Inside, the house looked raw and unfinished, though most of the furniture had been delivered. It was livable, but in the cold, damp weather, it seemed pretty uninviting.

"What's the weather going to do?"

"Supposed to clear up in a day or two, but you never know."

"I don't know about this, Richard," I said to myself as much as to him. "I'm not sure Frank ought to come down. Maybe I should just work around the place the rest of the day and drive home tomorrow."

"He'll be terribly disappointed if he doesn't get down here."

"Don't I know it."

I spent the rest of the day hanging curtains, making beds, and getting the kitchen in order. At 7 o'clock I drove into town and had a hamburger at Big Bob's. Then I went outside to the sidewalk telephone and called home. The wind had picked up. Standing there on the sidewalk with both a sweater and a windbreaker on, I got colder by the minute. I told Frank as much when he answered the phone. I also told him the cottage had no heat, no hot water, and no way to cook.

"We could eat out for a day or two. They'll get electricity in pretty soon, won't they?"

"They expect to."

"The weather can't stay cold for long this time of year."

"Well, it's cold now. I worry about your coming."

But Frank would not give up so easily. "I've waited so long to see that place—and I don't see why I should wait any longer just because the weather isn't perfect. After all, it isn't as if I have to *do* anything when I get there. I just want to sit and look at the view and read. I don't see what can go wrong."

So he drove down the next day, and the skies lightened somewhat. He climbed the stairs to the living room and drank in the scene of sky and water in muted greys etched with the white V's of the wings of seagulls and terns.

"Beautiful," he said.

Everything was going to be all right, I told myself. The weather would soon clear up, the workmen would get electricity in, and we would have a nice vacation. Frank would feel better at the end of it.

That night we had a thunderstorm. Rain poured down, and the temperature dropped 15 degrees. I dashed out in the car to the carry-out and brought back a soggy bag of hamburgers for dinner. Frank spent a miserable night trying to breathe in the cold, damp air. We wanted to drive home the next day, but he wasn't up to it, and anyway the roads were flooded.

Richard brought over an electric heater, and we spent the day huddled around it, watching it rain outside and watching the stains on the ceiling spread. The roof leaked. It confirmed our suspicion that the builder had cut a corner or two while we had been preoccupied with Frank's illness.

Next day the rain let up somewhat, and we decided to risk getting home in both cars. I warmed up Frank's car and slogged through the mud to the front door. If he felt too bad to go on, he was to pull over to the side of the road. I would follow and pick him up.

He got home all right. Then he called the doctor, who doubled his prednisone and sent him to bed for a week.

It was the end of something.

Not the end of trips to Chincoteague. We vacationed there—or attempted to—until the very end. In time the cottage had electricity, the Franklin stove worked, and the roof didn't leak. But Chincoteague is low, marshy, and humid. Unless the weather was ideal, Frank couldn't stay there very long. A lot of our vacations ended after two or three days with me hurriedly closing up the place, hurling our bags into the car, and driving off with Frank beside me gasping for breath and nervously spraying bronkosol into his lungs with the nebulizer.

It was a perfect cottage; the memories are bittersweet.

After one such vacation, Frank summed it up in a letter to a friend: "It is a sign of the last great ironist coming to mark against my name, of course, but all my life I've wanted a house in a marsh, and now that I've got one, I can't breathe in high humidity."

A lot of the Chincoteague vacations were disappointing, but none was as painful as that first one. I hadn't realized until we got home how much I had followed Frank's lead in thinking that everything would be all right if we could just get to our cottage there. But regardless of how Chincoteague had cast a spell over both of us, it held no magic reversal of his illness. The life we had dreamed of living there was never going to be. Not only that, but I was beginning to recognize a fundamental change in our relationship: I was beginning to be more caregiver than wife.

A Ceaseless Rain

I didn't admit all this to myself right away. Instead I went back to the office and buried myself in work. As we approached the long Fourth of July weekend, I felt a surge of panic that didn't ease up until I found a place for myself on a crash project requiring a huge amount of writing to be done by the Tuesday after the holiday.

"Why on earth did you allow yourself to get saddled with all that work over the long weekend?" Frank wanted to know.

I didn't tell him it was because I was afraid if I had three whole days in which to think, I would come apart.

Slowly Frank's illness narrowed our lives. Only on rare occasions did we go to plays or concerts; the effort required was simply too great to do it often. When we ate out, we choose unpretentious restaurants where I could drive Frank close to the door and we could leave easily if necessary.

We did not seek new friends, and not all of the old ones stuck with us. I remembered how sick people had always made me feel—so uncomfortable about not knowing what to do or say, so aware of being luckier—and so guilty about it and yet so worried that the luck might not last or that the bad luck might be contagious. Illness puts you in touch with your own mortality, and it can be scary. I understood. Frank, who still did not admit he was sick, did not. He felt hurt when old friends took weeks to return a phone call or rarely dropped in anymore.

What energy Frank had went into keeping the quality of *Defenders* as high as ever. For the limitations that illness imposed on him professionally, he found ways to compensate. Since he could not walk far to take photographs, he bought a 400-millimeter lens that brought distant subjects into range. Since his hands trembled from the medication, he set up tripods to hold his camera. Because he could not travel much, he wrote about what was close at hand, and he found a new eloquence in writing about the commonplace—a reed of marsh grass, the flight of a falcon, an ant on a dandelion. In his work, at any rate, there were a few small gains.

Everywhere else there were losses. Showering became an ordeal. If too much steam collected, he could not breathe. The effects of prednisone began to show: his once-thick hair thinned out. His feet and ankles were often so swollen he could not wear dress shoes, so he wore moccasins most of the time. As the muscles in his arms and legs weakened and shrank, he became correspondingly thicker in the middle. He grew a beard to conceal his heavy jowls. He looked awful.

We didn't sleep together anymore. As his breathing grew worse, I spent too much time lying awake in the dark listening to it. It left me tired without having accomplished anything, so I moved to an adjoining bedroom. Frank agreed that I should move, but it hurt his feelings when I did. To compensate a little, I would get up a few minutes early and slip into bed with him. That way he woke with my arm around him, and he liked that. And his sense of humor remained intact. He would mumble, "Hark, it's the dawn maiden," or some such nonsense.

I grieved about the change in Frank's appearance. He had been a handsome man, and I had been powerfully attracted to him physically. Now he had changed so much that I sometimes thought only the eyes were the same. My feelings changed a little—or, rather, new feelings came. While I often felt tenderness, I now sometimes felt—as I looked at the ravages of illness and listened to the constant gasping—little waves of revulsion.

I was ashamed of feeling this way, of course. The more I felt it, the harder I tried to hide it. At times like this, I tended to hover solicitously over Frank, and it annoyed him terribly.

It hurt to see what was happening to Frank. In the evening when I came home from work, I began to numb that hurt by having an extra scotch or two before dinner. It seemed to me one of the few things I could safely turn to. I had been a moderate drinker for thirty years and had rarely, if ever, abused alcohol. Now it seemed to bring a little relief from pain, and I saw no reason I should not use it for that purpose.

Chapter 7
To Undo Things Done

O God! O God! that it were possible
To undo things done; to call back yesterday!
Thomas Heywood, *A Woman Killed with Kindness*

By the end of the first year of Frank's illness, the question was not whether I would get through it nobly but whether I would get through it at all.

Frank was, in many ways, setting an inspiring example in how to face illness. He refused to give in to it, stayed in good spirits, never felt sorry for himself.

In contrast, I had already fallen miserably short of my goal of "grace under pressure." I considered it a failure on my part, but I could not control my mind and emotions as he did his. I was losing him—and I could not get my mind off that fact. Nor could I handle the emotions that came—grief, anger, self-pity. The harder I tried to keep my thoughts and feelings reined in, the more they spun out of control.

I began to worry about the odd things my mind did, almost independently of me. By fall of the first year, I had lost hope that Frank would get well. And now that my mind no longer had hope to play with, it began a strange new kind of compulsive thinking, the aim of which was to get Frank well another way—by reversing reality.

Over and over I replayed the key events that had led to Frank's illness, and I tried to change one of them. Part of my mind knew that what I was doing was crazy; the other part worked at it compulsively.

Frank's illness, as I saw it, had been caused by a series of minor events—coincidences, things of no importance in themselves. They were all hooked together, though, each one a link in the chain that led, inevitably, to his death. If only one of those links hadn't been there or had broken, Frank would still be well. So, somehow I would break one small link in that chain, and then he would be all right again. I decided to go over that chain in my mind until I saw its weak place and then break it. By concentrating hard, and through sheer force of will, I would force it to break. Somewhere, I was sure, there must be a very small link that would give way.

As if fingering a string of beads, I examined the series of events that had brought us where we were. If only Dr. McMinn hadn't treated the flu with ampicillin, to which he was allergic, Frank wouldn't have broken out in a rash; if there had been no rash, the doctor wouldn't have prescribed prednisone; if there had been no prednisone, the symptoms of the lung infection would not have been masked; if the infection had not been masked, the doctor would have realized how ill Frank was and would have insisted that he go to the hospital; if only Frank had entered the hospital earlier, he would have been treated and would not have gone for two months with an infection destroying his lungs. He would be well again. Not dying. He would be well again.

Sometimes I started further back in time and went over the events that led up to the flu. If only Frank hadn't been so eager to get the December issue of *Defenders* out on time that he asked the staff— including those with flu—to work on Saturday if they possibly could, then he wouldn't have worked with them all day nor driven them home afterward. He would never have caught flu at all. The final "if only" always brought a pang: if only they hadn't loved him so much, they wouldn't have come in.

These events ran through my mind like an old movie. When I got to a crucial place, I would stop the image and reverse the action. Sometimes I stopped the film where the doctor prescribed ampicillin. I changed it to some other drug, so then there was no rash, no prednisone, no hidden lung infection. Sometimes I changed it where the doctor prescribed prednisone. Without the prednisone, the doctor saw immediately that a lung infection had developed and he treated it, and Frank got well. Sometimes I stopped it where Frank ran out of the doctor's office. In these replays, the doctor told Frank to go to the hospital, and Frank went. Sometimes I changed my own behavior. I edited out all of my timid phone calls to the doctor and started with the final, firm one ("I'm taking Frank to the hospital"), thereby cutting almost three weeks off the time that the infection damaged the lungs.

Compulsively, endlessly, I went over the sequence of events and tried to stop them somewhere, anywhere. It didn't seem possible that one minor coincidence could follow another minor coincidence and that at the end of the line a man would be dying. All the things that had gone wrong were little things. Death was major. Nothing that terrible should be caused by all these little things. For months I picked up the chain every time I had a quiet moment and went over and over it, fumbling for the link that would break, wanting to believe, and half believing, that when something terrible happens that ought never to have happened, there must be a way to undo it.

On the whole, though, the times when my mind played "if only" were less disturbing that the times it took up another compulsive exercise: "Who's to blame?" The first only caught me in an endless cycle of frustration. The second tapped a seething cauldron of anger that was building just below the surface.

My anger found various targets. Sometimes it focused on the doctor. I blamed him for a good many things—for prescribing a powerful drug like prednisone for a rash, and then for forgetting that the drug can hide real trouble; for being so easily fooled into thinking that because Frank was witty, he couldn't be very sick; and for not taking me seriously when I tried to express my growing alarm to him. That rankled. He had been high-handed and, with his "busy doctor" manner, he had put me down.

I was more furious at myself, though, for letting him do it. I had known, deep down, that something was terribly wrong, and I had failed to get that warning across. I had let the doctor ignore my worries and treat me as if I were an empty-headed, hysterical female. I hated myself for letting him silence me. My life before all this was full of episodes when I had refused to be put down and had willingly created an uproar, if that was what it took, to be heard. What in hell had made me so hesitant about pressing my opinions on so vital an issue? By the time I took matters into my own hands and acted on what I knew, it was too late. I had no one to blame for that except myself.

Most of all, though, I raged against Frank. He had smoked heavily—and gone on smoking heavily—long after he was first told he had "a touch of emphysema." After he recovered from alcoholism, he continued to smoke because he thought smoking relieved some of the tension for which he had previously used alcohol. It was better to smoke than to drink, he said. With smoking, "at least you die with dignity."

I understood this but I didn't forgive it. With his heavy smoking, years of alcoholism, and refusal to admit it when he was sick, Frank had lived very self-destructively. And that—here my thinking took a self-centered turn—that hadn't been fair to *me*. I had finally found a man I could love completely, and after one year of marriage—just one—he was leaving me. Inch by excruciating inch he lost ground. I stood helplessly by, watching everything go—his looks, our love life, his physical strength, his ability to concentrate, our social life. Hope. Everything good was in the past. The future was unbearable to think about—an eon of days stretching out ahead of us, each one a little worse than the one before. I didn't know how to cope with this except to try to change it through my frantic little game of "if only."

Once, though, I tried another tack. Up the hill from our house lived 89-year-old John Wolfe. His wife had died more than five years earlier; except for a housekeeper who came in a few hours a week and occasional visits from his son, he had no one to look after him. He was a very nice man who once had been the mayor of University Park. Now, though, repeated strokes had much impaired his mind and body. When he took walks, he often could not find his way home. One day as I looked out of the window, Mr. Wolfe shuffled by. His winter coat was not buttoned properly; one side was down six inches from the other. He looked lost again.

"God," I thought, "please take him instead!"

It was one of the few times in Frank's long illness that I had anything to say to God. He didn't accept the deal, of course. I went on not believing in Him but being mad as hell at Him, anyway.

One of the few things that did work and did sometimes relieve the intensity of my feelings was to write in my journal. Onto its pages I poured the anguish and anger that I dared not express anywhere:

> Nov. 18
> Bad, restless night. I told Frank I never forgave him or the doctor for letting this happen. That opened the way for feelings that frighten me. I hate him, and his appearance, and what he has done to my life. I hate sickness. I don't want to spend my life with a sick man. I hate the breathing machines and the oxygen cylinders. I hate the sound of gasping. I hate myself for hating. I want to get out of this. I don't want to go through with what's ahead.

The anger spilled over into the job, making a difficult situation there much worse. I had had a bad break on my job. My supervisor, the man who had hired me, left for another job. The man who replaced him was a political appointee whose experience as vice president of a deviled ham company did not qualify him, so far as I could see, to be deputy director of the National Endowment for the Arts. In no time at all, I realized he knew nothing about publications, so I ignored him and went about my job. In no time at all he conceived an intense dislike for me. Shortly after he came on, he made it clear that one of the first things he would like to accomplish was to make my life so miserable I would leave.

His hostility was way out of proportion to anything I did or failed to do, and I never fully understood it. Perhaps some personalities are just bound to clash. Perhaps he sensed that something was terribly wrong. He never knew about Frank because I did not tell my problems in the office except to a few close friends, but the fallout of my trouble was easy to see. I was preoccupied and withdrawn. I tried to mask my inner turmoil with an outward appearance of calm, but the effect was one of cold efficiency and arrogance. Whatever it was, I disturbed the new man profoundly, and he desperately wanted to get rid of me.

I couldn't give up my job. I had no idea how much longer Frank could work, and we needed my income. His drugs alone cost more than $500 a month. Besides, I had no energy or emotional reserve for job-hunting. I decided to stay and take it.

C. D. Shoals (not his real name, of course) was out to destroy me. What I didn't want him to know was how easily I thought that could be done. Therefore, I was determined to show no weakness. Whatever he gave me, I would give back.

We set the pattern early. Shoals would bait me by doing or saying something outrageous. I would oblige by responding with rage. Once this pattern was set, the battle had its own momentum. One by one he called the members of my staff into his office and questioned them about me. No tale was too far-fetched for him to believe. One morning he burst into my office, his face flushed a bright red under his shock of white hair. "I want to talk with you about this umbrella-throwing episode," he shouted.

"What umbrella-throwing episode?" I shouted back.

"Ann Smith (not her real name, either) says you threw an umbrella at her."

"That's ridiculous. I don't even own an umbrella."

"You don't expect me to believe that, do you?"

"No. I wouldn't expect anything so intelligent of you," I yelled at him as he slammed out of the office.

"You're a bad manager," he shouted at me one day.

"It takes one to know one," I snapped back.

So it went. I never started one of our nasty exchanges, but I never handled one well, either. I always managed to give him fresh cause to loathe me.

"You've had a pick on me since the day you arrived," I said once. "You're conducting a personal vendetta against me."

"That's right," he said with a smirk. "What are you going to do about it?"

I considered for a moment, looked him straight in the eye, and rashly made the response that would infuriate him most. "I'm going to outlast you," I said.

"Oh, no, you're not," he said. "I'm going to start an adverse action on you. I'm going to fill out the papers right now," he shouted over his shoulder as he stomped out of the office.

He did it, too. But the adverse action, which is government-speak for firing, didn't get anywhere because there was nothing, really, to charge me with.

Once I had been very disciplined and professional on the job, and now I was completely reckless. I hated C. D. Shoals. I thought he was a dreadful bully, and I turned my fury on him with no thought of how I was damaging my reputation. I jeopardized a career I had spent years building, and the strange thing was that I didn't care. I was beginning to think of the job as something I needed only as long as it took to see

Frank through. After that, I didn't see any future, anyway. So the job didn't matter, and what people thought about me mattered even less.

Yet sometimes when we quarreled, I listened to my angry voice reverberating down the corridor and I felt disoriented, as if I were listening to someone else's voice, someone else's anger. I hated Shoals for finding my anger and bringing it out. I began to hate myself, too.

Not surprisingly, I got a reputation for being quick-tempered. Except for some loyal staff members and a few friends I had made before the trouble with Shoals broke out, people kept their distance and treated me warily. I saw that I was disliked and I regretted it. Under ordinary circumstances I could never have endured the isolation and hostility. But there is a level of emotional pain beyond which you cannot feel any more, and I had just about reached it.

Most of my life I had enjoyed work and had made good friends on the job. Now work, too, had become a kind of hell. I simply moved between two worlds where everything was going wrong.

I began to take longer lunch hours and to select companions who would linger with me over a second cocktail. Somehow, though, the extra drink did not give my spirits the expected lift. Instead, in the afternoons I was more depressed than ever.

I had always taken pride in my self-control and now, when I needed it, it was gone. Not only did I become angry when I would have given anything to stay calm, but I also began to cry a lot at unexpected times and places. I managed never to cry at work—I buried everything under anger there—but otherwise, I never knew when I would burst into tears or how long it would take to stop.

It wasn't like me. Or, rather, it wasn't like who I thought I was, or who I was pretty sure I used to be. Once I thought I knew myself quite well, but I didn't know this volatile, moody, angry person I had become.

One January day I met Jean, an old friend, for lunch. Her husband had died several years ago after a long illness. "Well, how are things?" she inquired kindly.

A little kindness was all I needed to set off a crying jag that went on and on while embarrassed customers averted their eyes and a waitress hovered uncertainly nearby wondering whether to ask for our order.

"I'm so sorry," I said. "I didn't mean to do this. Here in Garfinkel's tea room and everything."

"Garfinkel's be damned," said Jean. "Have a good cry."

When it was over, Jean suggested that I see a therapist. She had done that when her husband was dying, and it helped. She gave me a name to call and made a convincing case: "You have to pull yourself together if only for Frank's sake. You can't go on like this, you know."

I did know. I was trying everything I knew, but I wasn't making it, and I was running out of ideas to try. I hated admitting I couldn't handle everything by myself, but I swallowed my pride and placed the call.

Chapter 8
The Shadow of Death

*Though I walk through the valley
of the shadow of death...*

Bible, 23rd Psalm

"I was lying on the bed fully dressed with my hands clasped across my chest. The room was dark and very small—a long, narrow room like the spare bedroom at home. People came by and stood in the hallway and stared at me. I wanted to get up, but I seemed to be paralyzed. I could not move my hands or my feet, or even turn my head or change my expression. I wanted to cry out, but I couldn't make a sound. I knew I had urgent things to do, and it was wrong to be lying there, but I was helpless to do anything about it."

"What do you think the dream means?" Marc asked. Marc was the therapist I had called, and it was my second appointment. At my first one, he had asked me to write down any dreams I might have. I said that I could never remember them, and within the week had a dream I could not forget—one that woke me shivering with fright.

I took a stab at interpreting it. "I guess I'm late for work and can't get going—and I'm very anxious about it."

"No. The room is like a coffin. It's a dream about death."

"Of course. That's what brought me into therapy. Frank is dying, and I can't handle my feelings about it."

"No," he said. "You're the one in the coffin. You fear that you are dying, too."

It took a minute to recognize that he was right.

"Why do you fear you're dying?" he asked.

"Because I don't think I can go on," I said. "I'm so depressed all the time. I don't think I can get through this."

"Why else do you think you're dying?"

"Because I don't want to go on," I said finally. "I'm not going to have anything to live for." And then I broke into tears and spent the rest of the session crying.

It helped to say it, to get it out and cry about it. Week after week I went into Marc's office and said that my life was ruined, I couldn't stand any more, and I couldn't go on. And always I went home and made the best of the situation and went on.

From the first, I liked Marc and trusted him. He was a far cry from the scholarly, three-piece-suit type that I had expected. With his bushy black beard and intense eyes, he looked like a youthful version of an Old Testament prophet. He was in his late thirties, six feet three inches tall, and looked strong as an ox. I liked the immense physical strength. I felt that I could throw all of my troubles at him and they would not rock him, and I was right.

Therapy was my safety valve. I got a lot of crying done during that hour, and that helped me to stop erupting into tears at unexpected times and places. I poured out my hatred of sickness and sick people and breathing machines and hospitals. I talked about my fear that I would run dry—out of energy and resources—and would then do something terrible. I felt that I had it in me to do something terrible, and it scared me. As I talked about my anger and fears, they weren't my guilty little secrets any more. It helped immensely to have someone to whom I could express my honest feelings without fear of condemnation.

The fear of running dry had some basis in reality. In addition to a husband who was becoming more and more of an invalid, I also had a full-time job with many deadlines, a large house and yard to look after, a second home in Chincoteague, and assorted responsibilities as mother, stepmother, and daughter-in-law. In spite of the fact that we hired people to clean the house and mow the lawn, I worked awfully hard. Fortunately, I had always had good health and a lot of energy, but even so, fatigue became a constant problem. It gave rise to fulminations like this one in my journal:

> March 4
> God, I have to do everything that gets done, and I am so damned tired. I have to hold down my job as if I were only a part-time typist, take care of the house and yard, vacation when it works for *his* job, haul in the groceries, cook, haul out the garbage, do the laundry, pick up after him, keep both cars in repair, have his kids to dinner and drive them home afterwards.
>
> I don't get to read. I don't get any solitude. I don't do my job the way I want to do it—the way he does his, the way most men do theirs—because everybody has a claim on me. I feel so trapped. He is so calm and admirable. And I am so desperate.

But sometimes there was a new and calmer tone in the journal entries:

> May 4
> Chincoteague. It's good to be here. We've been through a lot of emotional hoo-rahs for many weeks, and it's good to get away. The months ahead will bring what they must, but I just slept nine hours and I'm rested—up at 6:30 to find the day clear and beautiful.

Not that everything is suddenly easy. Frank has increased his prednisone, sometimes doesn't seem like himself. Cranky. Everything is hard—packing, moving the medical equipment, timing the IPPB breathings between activities. Meals out are a little hard. He overeats, does more gasping than he knows. When I stop and think, I get sad. But I do have a better hold on things than I did—less depressed, less angry, more willing to live this day.

And then, just when I was learning to live without hope, hope came. As an experiment, Dr. Steinberg connected him to a tank of pure oxygen and asked him to walk a treadmill as long as he could. Frank walked—and walked—and walked—the equivalent of half a mile before he had to stop. The doctor was elated. He called me in from the waiting room and told me what had happened. "One in a hundred responds that way," he said.

He explained that new technology now made it possible for a patient to carry his own oxygen with him in a portable oxygen tank. He phoned Oxygen Therapy, Inc., a medical supply firm, and arranged for someone to come out to the house with the latest equipment and instruct Frank in its care and use.

Frank was ecstatic. "This is the breakthrough that will change our lives," he said. "I'll be able to go where I want to go. I can meet people for lunch, walk the trails in Chincoteague, even walk the ocean beach with you again. The quality of air won't matter. I'll carry mine with me." Right there in the doctor's office he wrapped his arms around me and gave me a big kiss.

My spirits soared. I could scarcely believe how lucky we were—one in a hundred! A reprieve had been granted. I would have something of the old Frank back, something of the life we once had together. At least for awhile.

Next morning a technician from Oxygen Therapy brought out the new equipment—a "cow" and a "walker." The "cow" weighed sixty-five pounds and contained the basic supply of oxygen. The "walker," which weighed only twelve pounds, could be filled with an eight-hour supply of oxygen and worn from the shoulder.

"That's the same stuff they use to launch rockets," said the technician proudly.

"Well, it ought to get me moving again, then," Frank responded.

We couldn't wait to try it. When he filled the "walker," we hung it on Frank's shoulder and agreed that it looked just like a piece of luggage. We didn't mention that luggage does not have a green plastic tube, or cannula, that goes into the bearer's nose. That was a minor distraction, hardly worth mentioning.

It came as a shock to discover that the oxygen had no effect at all on what Frank could do. He became short of breath, as usual, in five minutes. We could not quite believe it that first day. Perhaps, we thought, tomorrow, after a good night's sleep, he'll do better. But it made no difference then, either. No one could ever explain how it happened that one day in the doctor's office Frank walked half a mile while breathing pure oxygen, because he never could do it again. The only difference the oxygen made was that Frank felt worse if he stopped breathing it for long. So for the rest of his life Frank usually had a plastic tube in his nose and was never far from the "cow" or "walker."

Each of us hid our bitter disappointment from the other. Neither of us ever talked about how painful it had been to have hopes built up so high and then to have them dashed.

Gone were the days when Frank could mix with a crowd and not stand out as sick. Now his pallor, his slow gait, the soft slippers that he usually wore, the sound of his breathing, and especially the dangling, green cannula testified to his invalidism. He hated people making way for him and treating him solicitously. When we were in public, I practiced looking unconcerned about him, even indifferent.

I was fiercely protective, though. Once in a restaurant, a little girl about five years old caught sight of the cannula. "Look, Mama," she said, tugging at her mother's skirt. Frank hadn't heard, and the mother hadn't turned, so I decided to silence her before she said it again. I fixed on her a glare perfected years earlier as a high school English teacher. It silenced them then, and it silenced her now. She quickly took refuge behind her mother's skirt. No one stared at Frank if I could help it.

I knew Frank was losing ground, but I did not realize what a paper-thin margin he operated on until one day in September. We had taken off for a week in Chincoteague, each of us with a stack of papers to edit. For once, we hit a perfect spell of warm, dry weather, and Frank savored every minute of the time. He was so happy, in fact, that he ignored the minor discomfort of an infected cyst on his thigh.

Midway through the week, the infection became too painful to ignore but it didn't seem serious enough for us to interrupt our vacation. Infections require antibiotics; we didn't need a doctor to tell us that. Frank had a prescription for tetracycline. He refilled it and started on a moderate dose. He decided to give the infection one day to respond; if it didn't, we would go home and Frank would see his doctor. We invited some friends over for dinner that night, and Frank seemed happier than he had been in weeks.

Next morning, I couldn't get him up. He opened his eyes, smiled, mumbled a few words, and fell asleep again. He's just tired, I thought. I'll let him sleep. But I grew increasingly apprehensive. Every half hour or so I tried to wake him. By ten o'clock I realized that he was getting less responsive and that his breathing seemed shallower. I was sure something was wrong.

My first thought was to get him back to Washington where his doctors were. I decided to pack everything in the car and park it close to the door. Then I would force him to wake up enough to get in the car. He needed to walk only about ten yards. I thought that if I could just get him on his feet, we could make it.

The Shadow of Death

Too late. When I tried to rouse him, Frank only mumbled incoherently. I tried to get him to sit up, but he was a dead weight. I couldn't possibly move him. Apprehension gave way to panic as I suddenly realized that I had an emergency on my hands and was running out of time to deal with it.

Chincoteague, Virginia: One doctor. Nearest hospital: Salisbury, Maryland, 50 miles away.

I called the doctor. His nurse told me that he had just left town for the day. Desperate, I called our architect friend, Richard, who thought the doctor might be heading for the golf course on his afternoon off. If so, he had to be driving on Main Street toward the bridge—the only way off the island.

"I'll try to cut him off," Richard shouted as he slammed down the phone.

Richard told me later how close it had been. As he sprinted for the main road, he spotted the black Cadillac approaching. Just in time, he ran out into the road with his arms outstretched and blocked its path. The doctor slammed on the brakes and swore.

Minutes later, Richard and the doctor pulled into the driveway in front of the cottage. The doctor was not happy at having been shanghaied into making a house call. His mood was surly; he communicated an attitude of "this better be good."

"What is wrong with your husband?" he asked in a bored tone as we walked toward the cottage.

"He has emphysema," I said.

"What seems to be the problem now?"

"He's unconscious. I think he's dying. I don't know why."

We said no more until we reached the cottage. His manner changed when he saw Frank. He was all efficiency and concern.

"What medications is he taking?"

"Forty milligrams of prednisone, five milligrams of brethine twice a day, two-and-a-half milligrams of bronkosol four times a day through the IPPB, a measured dose of vanceril three times a day, 60 milligrams of lasix, and three klorvess tablets."

"Holy shit," he said softly.

He did a quick examination. "It's the cyst that's causing the problem."

"How can that be?"

"The infection is burning up all the oxygen. He doesn't get all that much. And the prednisone has made the infection systemic."

He phoned for an ambulance, and he spoke to a doctor at Salisbury hospital and told him to expect Frank. Then he packed his bag and got ready to go. "He'll be in the hospital in an hour. He's not going to die before then." He took my hand. "Goodbye," he said. "I'm glad you caught me."

"I'm glad, too. Thanks for everything."

He looked at Frank. "How old is this man?"

"Fifty."

"Shit," he said sadly and almost inaudibly. Then he got in his car and drove off.

At the hospital, doctors lanced the cyst—and kept Frank for two weeks until the level of oxygen in his blood rose. Frank acknowledged that he had had a brush with death, but he did not acknowledge that his illness was therefore serious. He regarded the problem with the cyst as a fluke and continued to plan and live as if he would soon be better.

There was a lot of love between us, but there were a lot of strains on that love because the illness created conflicting needs. Frank needed to continue to deny its seriousness. I needed to confront the situation honestly and talk about it. I wanted to ask him what I should do if he died. I wanted to know if in his heart he was still a Catholic and wished to be buried as one. I wanted to know if he had made a will. I wanted to stop pretending that being on constant oxygen wasn't a serious sign of something. I wanted him to help me face the fears I had of being alone, and I wanted to help him face his fears.

Only once was I able to get him near the subject of dying—and that was by discussing not his death, but mine. "Frank," I said one day. "If I should predecease you, I want you to know this: I'd like to be cremated and have the ashes scattered in a body of water that is going somewhere interesting—maybe Assateague Bay or Chesapeake Bay. I'd like a memorial service, and I'd like Wofford Smith [our neighbor and an Episcopalian priest] to conduct it."

"OK."

"How about you?"

"I guess that would do for me, too."

Except for this exchange, whenever we veered close to the subject of dying, Frank became so downcast that I would drop the subject. We could talk easily and honestly about many things, but on the huge, overriding subject of his illness and its implications, we could not communicate.

I had always thought of Frank as wiser and steadier than I, and I counted on his help in solving problems. Now his illness posed problems that seemed overwhelming. My instinct was to turn to him for guidance, but he was not there. He could not admit any problems.

I wanted to be appreciated, too. Despite outbursts of anger and tears, I was always there when he needed me. I wasn't always pleasant and agreeable (though often I was), and I was a far cry from the uncomplaining wife I wanted to be—in fact, he accused me of complaining a blue streak, and there was some truth in it. Still, I hadn't run, and I hadn't let him down. I was hurting a lot. He couldn't understand why.

Later, it made sense to me. If he could not admit that he was ill, then he certainly could not see the toll that illness took on me or anyone else. But I didn't understand it at the time. I only knew that his illness did not bring us closer together as I hoped it would. Instead, it drove us apart in a hundred different ways.

CHAPTER 9
The Wine Cup of This Fury

> Take the wine cup of this fury at my hand. . . .
> *Bible, Jeremiah 25:15*

It was in the expression of emotion that Frank and I were furthest apart. He could no more reveal his than I could contain mine. I knew that he disliked intense emotion, but I also knew that I could not keep my emotions bottled up. When I tried, they simply exploded with unexpected force at unexpected times. Instead, I tried to get them out in weekly therapy sessions, talk them over with friends, or write about them in my journal.

But I had a terrible problem with anger, particularly in the second year of Frank's illness. I was certain then that he could not live long. I knew it, but I could not accept it. Each bit of new evidence that I was losing him made me furious. I took it personally, angrily.

Once Frank said to me, "Marcia, you're a wonderful woman in so many ways, and I love you dearly, but I have never, never known anyone with so much anger inside."

It was a fair assessment. The journal shows that regardless of how hard I tried to control my emotions and how helpful therapy and friends were, nevertheless, in the second year, anger and despair built to a tremendous crescendo that erupted one day with destructive fury.

Feb. 11
Today I came home from work so tired and so much needing to be with Frank. But he was so fidgety from all the medications that he couldn't hold still. His hands and feet tapped all the time, and with trembling hands, he stroked his beard. This is not really the man I married.

Feb. 22
The basic problem remains the same—how to live with Frank, help him through this, and keep my own spirits up. The most distressing thing right now is that he is changing so much—not only in looks but in personality.

April 26
I'm realizing that I'm like my mother in one fundamental way—my anger is like hers—highly emotional, intense, furious, with elements of martyrdom, self-pity, and destructiveness. I have violent outbursts of truth-telling, telephone slamming, and so on. It takes a frightful emotional toll on everyone.

May 22
Chincoteague. The end of a wretched vacation. Ten days of rain. I moved heaven and earth to get here, left the office at a bad time because it was a good time for Frank, wasn't home when Dan came back for vacation. Now I feel cheated—nothing but rain, and I have used all my annual leave.

It makes me think how badly my life is working out. I don't want to stay in wet, rainy Chincoteague, but

I also don't want to go back to Washington and face all that trouble on the job. So I don't want to go and I don't want to stay. And I don't even much want to be. I realize that Frank is my anchor to life, or so it seems. I realize how fragile my hold on life is, or so it seems. I think in one of these black moods I could one day end it all.

Tell Frank something like this, and he says, "So it rains on you, and you want to go shoot yourself. What kind of sense does that make?" He doesn't like the gloom and the despair and the complaining. He doesn't like me when I am miserable, and he goes away. It's nothing against me, he explains, but he is still vulnerable, and if he hurts too much, he could drink again.

He's right. I'm terribly negative, bitter, cheated. I feel that this may be our last vacation here, and we are both paying dearly for it and not getting it.

I can never be cheerful enough for Frank, though. God knows, I admire the spirit he has about his illness. He will not quit. He doesn't let it get him down. But I do not have that kind of disposition. Now if I have problems he doesn't like, he rejects me. He doesn't love me when I'm depressed.

July 1
I'm 50 today. I hate landmark days of any kind, and I have particularly hated today.
I cannot cope any longer with my feelings about his appearance. His waist has gone from 38 to 54. He

doesn't shave; he doesn't get haircuts. The liquid oxygen makes his nose run, and it's cold and he can't feel it. The goddamned prednisone has destroyed his body, his muscles, his bones, his looks.

And, God, he was such a handsome man.

July 2

I have got to find a way to give Frank what he needs and not be destroyed in the process.

July 17

I am in a real depression. I cannot stand watching this man die by inches. I love him. I cannot stand the thought of what our future life together will be like. And yet I have to stand it. There is no way out.

Aug. 10

How callous I am much of the time. I'm surrounded, it seems, by the sounds of illness and pain. I am even beginning to complain to Frank about how much time he spends groaning.

Sept. 7

Our yard man couldn't come, so I mowed the lawn today. When I came in, I felt pretty good about it. But it made Frank feel useless and depressed. Sometimes you just can't win.

Frank is now very dependent on me. Neither of us likes that.

I am beginning to think how I will put my life together when Frank dies. Then he's still here. I should be glad I still have him. Most of the time I am.

Sept. 14
Recent photos of Frank most depressing and painful to look at. . .

There isn't any God, or he wouldn't have done that to Frank. . .

If I were Frank, I wouldn't like me. For one thing, I come home, take one look at what illness has done to him, and head for the bottle of Scotch. I get as numb as I can.

It's a mean world and lots of times I would be so glad to be out of it. Frank says he can't see much reason, either, for staying around.

When I really think about it, I know I'm not going to kill myself. Not now, anyway. I have some long-range interests—what's going to happen to Dan? To others? Frank says less about it, but means it more, I think.

Oct. 12
I can't keep my spirits up with Frank as he is. Depression or escape seem the only logical reactions. He has so many nervous twitches and spasms from drugs that it's hard to sit there and talk to him. I tried to talk cheerfully—said that after the boys all graduate from college, we will have a real vacation for ourselves. But he

jerks and gasps and breaks into a sweat and starts his nebulizer treatment. It's just so awful and so sad.

Oct. 18
I have to face how much I want this to end. There's not much of a relationship any more. Frank doesn't listen, doesn't care. I don't blame him. He likes me when I'm kind and do things that make his life easier. He is not able to do much more than carry on.

Nov. 5
Frank is totally self-absorbed. Not the man I married. How I hate him for letting this happen. Hate the doctor for letting it happen. Hate myself.

Nov. 19
It isn't going to happen that Frank will die while this marriage is still good and while I can feel good about the way I got through it. All the love is going to go, and I am going to wish it to be over with greater intensity all the time.

Dec. 3
He is talking about living ten more years—that's what Dr. Steinberg gave him. Dear God! I can't take ten more years of this, and yet I may have to.

We have no good years left. I don't think I can take ten years of looking after an invalid. I do not think so. No one really knows, but Dr. Steinberg kept someone alive—bedridden and on oxygen for six years. He thought I would be pleased to hear it.

The Wine Cup of This Fury

Dec. 10
God I hate sick people. I hate Frank, I hate him I hate everybody.

Am I losing my mind? I want to smash something. Drive a car and crash. Die. Kill someone.

I hatehate hate. I'm trapped and I'm furious. He's so sick. He can't help me, and I'm desperate.

The climax of this build-up of anger was precipitated by a meeting that ought to have dissipated some of it. Early in December Marc thought it might help me to talk to a grief therapist, and he put me in touch with Emily, a woman who had lost her son several years earlier and who belonged to a volunteer organization that helped people face their own death or that of a loved one. Emily was a psychiatric nurse by profession and a gracious, understanding woman by temperament. Eventually it did help to talk with her, but our first meeting was prelude to a minor explosion.

It was not Emily's fault. She couldn't have been kinder or more willing to put herself out to help me, a total stranger. When I couldn't find a time to go to her home office, she offered to come to mine during lunch hour. We considered going out to lunch and decided that, with the kinds of things we wanted to discuss, it would be better just to talk.

I liked her. There was an air of serenity about her that I knew had been won the hard way. I found it easy to talk to her. The problem was that Emily needed to know my whole story. I had been trying not to look back or look ahead, but to live "one day at a time." That was the most useful of any of the platitudes I had come across.

Now, though, Emily needed the whole picture. And as I told it to her, I relived it all, and all the emotions came back. Then, because I was in the office and had to go on working and seeing people, I choked them all down.

We were too busy for me to get lunch that day. When I got home, I was hungry and exhausted, both physically and emotionally. I reached for the Scotch bottle for a quick pick-up. I had one drink, and then another, and then all the tears that I had choked down at noon came back. The pent-up grief and rage and despair broke through with a force I had never known. The pain of it clutched at the back of my throat and stabbed between my ribs. I ran upstairs to our study and tried to relieve the pain by writing about it.

> Dec. 16
> Oh, God, Frank is dying and I'm so angry at him. He brought this on himself. He and that doctor, who didn't have to be so stupid and slow.
>
> Now my life is just ruined and I'm dying too from the pain of it.
>
> I am not going to spend the rest of my life suffering for the mistakes of two stupid men.
>
> I will get a gun. And I will shoot Frank. If I do not do this, he will go on and on and on. I will be worn down to nothing . . . .
>
> I can't kill him. Killing him will kill me. I am chained to illness and death. Goddamn it! There is nothing I can do to express my rage! Nothing is violent enough!

Writing did not stem the gathering fury that seemed to have a life of its own. I got up from the desk and started pacing the room, heaving great noisy sobs and screaming the worst curses I could think of. That didn't help, either.

I wanted to do something violent. I had an overwhelming urge to break, smash, destroy. I looked around for something to break. I picked up the desk chair and hurled it with all my strength against the opposite wall. "Goddamn it!" One leg snapped off. The chair had gouged a hole in the wall the size of a dinner plate. I picked up what was left of the chair and hurled it again. And again. "Goddamn it! Goddamn it!"

Now there were two jagged holes in the wall. Chunks of plaster lay amid a pile of plaster dust on the floor. The chair lay in pieces. Nothing left to smash there.

I looked around for something else to destroy, seized Frank's chair, and threw it. The back broke. Sweating, and sobbing, and cursing, I threw it again and again until it lay in fragments with the other chair. I was drenched with sweat, gasping for air, utterly spent.

The storm was over.

Then I sat down on the floor of the study and cried quietly for a long, long time.

Do Not Go Gentle

A lone egret stands in Chincoteague Bay with the Assateague lighthouse in the background.

Chapter 10
A Calmer Grief

> Calm is the morn without a sound,
> Calm as to suit a calmer grief...
> Alfred, Lord Tennyson. *In Memoriam*

Outrageous as the episode was, it got rid of something toxic. Never again did my anger erupt with such fury or destructiveness.

As the third year of Frank's illness began, I became less stridently angry and more quietly despairing. At the same time, watching the number of good days dwindle, I developed a new ability to seize a good moment and squeeze every bit of happiness from it. In general, I became less sensitive to the sights and sounds of illness. Frank's gasping as he struggled up a flight of stairs less often tore at my heart; I went on with what I was doing. Yet sometimes I felt a new tenderness toward him. On our third anniversary I noted the dichotomy in my journal:

> Jan. 1
> Every day I clasp Frank to me as more precious than ever; and every day I prepare to part with him. It is a conflict of emotions more exhausting than I could ever have imagined.

On the job, though, I got a welcome reduction in conflict and emotion. The two-year feud with C. D. Shoals reached its climax when he burst in unexpectedly one morning.

"Do you remember the time you said you would outlast me?"

"Yes."

"I'm not going to let you do it. I'm going to fire you."

"You already tried it and nothing happened."

"I didn't follow through hard enough. This time I will."

I surprised myself by not shouting back. Instead I had an icy calm. "This time I'm not going to take any more. If you do one more thing to me, I'm going to the Civil Service Commission and file a grievance against you on the grounds of harassment. I ought to have done it months ago." Once I had said it, I realized I meant it.

He realized it, too. Within two days I was reassigned to another deputy, an intelligent and fair-minded young woman who did not hold my past against me. We established, first, a business-like relationship; and as the weeks went by, we added trust. Soon we liked and enjoyed each other. It changed my entire work life to have such a supervisor. It would take me years to erase the widespread image of myself as the Dragon Lady and replace it with something gentler, but that was all right. I regarded the job as going satisfactorily again, and that freed me to devote more energy to Frank.

Another helpful change occurred when Cris decided to spend the last semester of his senior year in the basement apartment of our house. It cheered Frank to have him around. They had long literary discussions, and each liked to read what the other had written and offer advice. And I appreciated having a strong young man around the house.

Prednisone had so softened Frank's bones that one January day he rolled over in bed and broke a rib. Taping or any sort of binding was out of the question since it would constrict his breathing. He simply endured the discomfort till the rib mended, and he moved more cautiously, always, after that.

He began having spells of insomnia at night and drowsiness during the days. The periods when he could concentrate on his work became shorter. I confided my growing alarm to the doctor.

Feb. 24
Dear Dr. Steinberg:
I must tell you what I cannot say in front of Frank. He is much worse. His mind isn't as it used to be. Much of the time he is somewhere between sleeping and being awake— or between being conscious and unconscious. He starts to tell me something but sometimes babbles off into nothing.

He is turning blue. His fingertips are always blue, even when he is on oxygen. He has terrible edema in his feet and ankles. Sometimes he cannot even get his feet into slippers.

A great change has taken place in the last two weeks. I don't know what to do. I need to have some understanding of what has happened so I can make some decisions. If he is going to stay this way, he should quit his job. It's unfair to hold on to a job with deadlines.

I need to know whether the time has come to get a practical nurse to help care for him. I need to know if he is going to live for five or ten years this way or if, as I suspect, he is going fast.

I would like to call and discuss these things with you.

The doctor's phone call shed light on these concerns. No, there was no brain damage; but because Frank could not get enough oxygen, he would sometimes be unable to concentrate. There might also be periods of disorientation. The worsening edema indicated trouble with his heart, something to be expected in this illness. There were many strains on his heart—insufficient oxygen in his blood, the strain of trying to breathe with lungs that had lost their elasticity, the pressure from hard coughing. No, the time had not yet come to hire a practical nurse although it might be close at hand. And, yes, Frank could live another five years although that was unlikely.

But it was the beginning of the end. Frank sensed it, too, and acknowledged it one day in his way: "I'm a very lucky man," he told me. "When I die, I'll be mourned and loved and well-bespoke. There was a time when that wouldn't have been true."

On a Sunday afternoon early in March, after Frank had been somewhat disoriented for two days, Cris and I took him to the hospital. He entered in the way that became "normal" for him—through the emergency room. The doctor met him there and, after beginning some medications, took him to a room.

Early Monday morning, before I went to work, I went by to see him. He was very drowsy, but that did not worry me too much. He didn't call me at work, though, and that did begin to worry me.

After work I drove to the hospital and hurried to his room. For a minute I thought I had the wrong room. The bed was empty. All of his clothes were gone. His papers were gone. A nurse was stripping the bed. There was no sign that Frank had ever been in this room. No, said the nurse, she didn't know where he was. She had just been told to change the bed.

I felt the bottom drop out of my world. No. You can't just lose a person. Frank must have died. I'm sure he died. But why didn't they call me? Why doesn't someone know where he is?

"He has to be somewhere," I said, trying to be calm. "Where do they take patients who. . ."

Suddenly the patient in the next bed roused himself. "You looking for Frank? They came by about an hour ago and took him to intensive care."

"Dr. Curtis is on his case," the nurse told me when I arrived at the intensive care station. "You can't come in now; but if you wait, Dr. Curtis will come out and talk to you."

I took a seat in the waiting room as close to the door to the intensive care unit as I could get. I wanted to be able to read the names on the badges of the doctors as they went in and out. That way, if Dr. Curtis couldn't find me, I could find him.

A lot of things can go through your mind in four hours. I realized that if Frank was in such bad condition that he needed intensive care, he might die. As the hours went by without a report from the doctor, I began to think that he probably was dying. I thought I couldn't stand it if he did. I wasn't ready for it. It had come too fast. I reminded myself that terrible things happened whether or not I was ready for them, so I had better prepare myself to hear the worst. I wished that I had asked Frank more about what he wanted me to do when he died. We never talked about religion. He always said he had left the church when he was eighteen and didn't think about religion much. I didn't think about it, either.

It occurred to me that if he didn't die and I had to hold a long vigil outside the intensive care unit again, I would bring something with me to eat.

I decided that if Frank died, I would accept it and be glad that he had been spared further suffering.

Then the doctor came out and told me that Frank was going to make it and I could see him, and I burst into tears of gratitude. There was no transition from one mood to the other. Four hours of preparing myself to face his death vanished into relief that, for now at least, he was all right.

A few minutes later, I walked for the first time into the awesome world of the intensive care unit. It is a shattering experience to walk through this room, looking at each face, searching for the one you love. There is something almost surreal in seeing so much suffering concentrated in one place. The sight of it is endurable only because one senses that the air is almost electric with alertness—alert machines, alert doctors and nurses, concentrating, responding instantly to what the machines and tests and patients tell them.

Frank was hooked up to an assortment of devices. An oxygen mask covered his mouth and nose. From discs pressed to his chest little wires ran to a black machine where jagged green lines blipped across the screen every few seconds. Plastic bags of colorless medicines hung on stands and dripped slowly into his arms through big plastic needles. They had had trouble getting the needles to stay in. Bloody bandages were taped down over the needles, and one arm was strapped to a board to prevent him from moving and dislodging the needle again.

I put one hand on his arm carefully in order not to dislodge anything. With the other hand I got a good grip on the side of the bed and held on. My legs had turned rubbery, and the room tilted at an odd angle. "For heaven's sake, you've never fainted, so don't start now," I told myself. "There is no soft furniture here. There is not even a place to fall." Gradually the room righted itself.

"You're going to be all right," I told Frank, "and I love you very much."

Under the oxygen mask he smiled at me.

After a few minutes, I left. It was past midnight when I got home, but the phone was ringing as I walked in. It was my mother-in-law, and she wanted a miracle.

"How is Frank tonight?"

"They put him in intensive care, Marj, but he's going to make it. He's not going to die."

"He has to do better than just make it. He has to get well."

"I wish I thought that could happen, Marj, but you know as well as I do that emphysema doesn't go away. Anyway, look at the way Frank is going through this. He is a kind of miracle. And we've still got him. We better be grateful for what we have."

"No, sir, he's got to get well. We need a miracle."

I agreed that a miracle was what it would take.

"It's up to you. Get down on your knees and pray for a miracle. You can do it if you have faith enough."

"Marj, I'm tired and hungry and I'm doing the best I can. I haven't been to church in twenty-five years. If there is a God, I'm not in touch. If you want to pray for a miracle, go ahead. But don't bother me with this."

"If you loved him, you'd do that for him. It's your fault if he dies."

In a way, though, we did get our miracle. Frank came out of the hospital three weeks later with such a heightened awareness of beauty and such a capacity to seize whatever joy might come his way that it was almost as if his life had expanded rather than narrowed. He wrote a column about it for *Defenders* magazine, and his own words tell this part of the story best:

> Eight inches of snow weighted down the ground and the spirit when Marcia and Cris trundled me into the hospital. When I walked shakily out again, the month of March had been used up, the snow was gone, and the crocuses nodded, already a little past their prime.
>
> I will spare you my hospital tale (although its slightest word would freeze your blood). Enough to state that for three-and-a-half weeks I roosted on one of those beds that are waterproof first and comfortable second, whose skirts hide a battery of engines designed to toss you up and down for the convenience of the doctors and nurses.

I was happy enough to leave that eighth-floor roost, where for company I had Mr. Walters, who would neither speak nor feed himself.

I wanted to see something growing, something beautiful in its rightness, something to look at that was perfectly proper to its living space. I know where the bald eagle soars and the snowy egret plumes, and I thought of going there—and took to my home bed for a week. When I had regathered both ounces of my strength, Marcia and I went out into a day that had been sent for me by the Eldar, or Someone.

Never was there such a day. Actually, never were there two such hours, which was all the day I could handle. But I rather suspect that I saw some things that my neighbors overlooked. They probably noticed the forsythia. Ha! Noticing isn't enough. It won't do. The absolute type specimens of the species, those against which all others should be measured, grew in yellow swaying provocation on every side.

Clumsy afoot, I almost flattened the very apotheosis of dandelions. Upon full and admiring study, this princely bloom displayed its secret: it was harboring a resplendent ant, all gloss, legs, feelers, easing the spring in its own way.

Marcia and I drove to a small park, where a majestic sycamore stood so whitely against the so-blue sky that I can see its singular angularity now, if I close my eyes. Then, as the car moved, the stony sycamore seemed to draw across its face a greening veil of weeping willow branches—the only tree we saw putting forth leaves. I am ashamed for my fellow citizens, but I must report they were walking by without pausing there for delight or instruction.

When we moved on, it was not to leave the trees, but boastfully to move—50 yards on foot was a marathon distance; conquered, it demanded a prize. Was ever half-smoke so bought? Was ever half-smoke so enjoyed? After a bland eternity among the low-sodium pastes of a hospital diet, that half-smoke, illicitly salty, presumptuously plump and juice-squirting, tasted better than filet mignon or oysters.

On a little pond there was a large duck. A down-at-the-heels, panhandling mallard (it seems now, from here; at the time he was a wonder). His iridescent green head turned royal purple in the sun as he begged bits of bun from us godlike half-smoke eaters. I have seen the trumpeter swan and the white pelican, and I wouldn't trade.

And there was an absolute dog. Black, more or less; big, sort-of; muddy, forepaws only; this splendid mammal lolloped about, carrying the good word from bench to bench, offering to give anybody a licking. It occurred to me that he should be assigned to a hospital. A dog is the essence of all the inefficient, friendly, germy help that hospitals hate. But I bet each would send more patients out through the front door if it kept a mutt or two to make rounds, thrust his muzzle in your ribs and say, "Hey, Hoss, what's with you? You feel lousy? Tell me all about it."

That would have cheered me, but just meeting one galloping free with his message in the free air was healing. My experience suggests to me that if I can get that sort of vivification from a dog or an ant or a dandelion, or the crinkled intricacy of a winter leaf skeleton, or a piece of mountain-range tree bark, I should be smart enough to do it without getting sick first. I think I'll try.

Chapter 11
Surprised by Joy

Surprised by joy—impatient as the wind...
William Wordsworth *Surprised by Joy*

Something of Frank's ability to find joy in small things and events began to rub off on me, for that spring, in spite of everything, there were times when life was sweet.

> April 7
> Frank and I both feel that we have been given a gift of time. The illness could have gone either way this time; in fact, I think the odds were that he would not pull through. Everything that we have before us now is a gift. "We're playing with the house money," Frank says. It would be foolish to squander it.

> April 12
> Chincoteague. We drove down here yesterday on a perfect spring day. The pear trees a haze of white blossoms, pink and red outlines around the branches of other trees. Forsythia is out, and willows. Frank was exuberant at the beauty of it all.

And our house—so beautiful, so right for its setting, so stunning in its view.

Then, the usual routine: a drink at our dining room table while we watched the 4 o'clock light warm and mellow the marsh grasses—the view a marvel of alternating water and marsh grass till finally Assateague Bay blends into the blue sky; then a drive around the refuge's inner loop—no ospreys sighted this time, but lots of Canada geese, terns, ducks; then a drive to the ocean; and for dinner, a flounder stuffed with crabmeat. A crazy flicker is trying to build a nest in our metal chimney. Frank says it sounds like a J. Arthur Rank production when he gets going, and has named the bird "old blunt-beak."

Frank said he lay awake last night for a long time not wanting to let go of the day, it was so good.

And today more routine things: a good breakfast and the decoy exhibition, where we each bought a decoy for the other (mine is an oyster catcher with a bright orange beak) and Frank bought small Canada geese decoys for everyone on his staff. And all the while Frank did so well—he was walking and talking at the same time—and so interested in everything, so *alive*. He took pictures of the decoy carvers and glass blowers and made notes for a column on decoy carving as a folk art.

These days are so good for Frank and for me. When he was in the hospital, something changed. We both learned a little about dying, and a lot about living.

April 15
Yesterday—another great one. I bought a peck of oysters, and we ate every one. Then we built a fire and sat on the couch watching it for a couple of hours. I didn't run off and work; Frank didn't read. We enjoyed the fire and being together.

Last night there was a fierce wind. The chimney groaned and squeaked; the outdoor vent on the range flapped; various parts of the house howled and whistled. After several hours of this, Frank remarked, "It *is* rather like living inside an oboe, isn't it?" I suggested that if we were going to have that much sound in the chimney, perhaps we could get it tuned.

That vacation was the last time we had entire days that were good. After that, we had some good afternoons or evenings when, for some reason, the symptoms would abate and Frank would breathe more easily and have a little energy. On those occasions we would drive someplace beautiful—usually to favorite spots near Washington, such as Greenbelt Park or Rock Creek Park, and play our photography game. We each had a camera, and we competed to see who could take the best pictures—under the new rules. These varied, according to how Frank felt, but generally we played twenty-twenty—which meant that we had twenty minutes to take pictures, and we could go as far as twenty steps from the car. On a good day, we might play thirty-thirty; and once, when Frank shouldn't have been out at all, we played five-five.

The game sharpened my awareness of beauty in small things, but Frank always won the contest hands down. It was he who saw the geometry of a spider's web, the spiky beauty of thistles, the loneliness of a gull flying into the fog, the tiny drama of a leaf caught in a swirling eddy. Sometimes he saw the picture, but couldn't get it because his hands trembled too much. On those occasions I took the picture but we counted it his. He had an exceptionally good eye for beauty. It had surprised me at first to find that this man, who could be so genuinely funny, often took photographs whose mood was lonely and melancholy. I, on the other hand, with an innately more melancholy nature, took photos of glorious sunsets and cheery beach scenes. I resolved to try to see things more through Frank's eyes, partly because it was better photography and partly because it might be a way that some of Frank's talent could go on.

Frank began to have trouble sleeping at night. He would fall asleep and then wake a few hours later; the rest of the night he would sit on the edge of the bed and tried to hold himself erect. If he dropped off to sleep while sitting up, he would wake as his head fell forward and pull himself erect. Toward morning, he would lie down and sleep again. I couldn't understand it. It was as if he felt that staying upright was a matter of life or death.

"He does feel that it's a matter of life or death," the doctor explained, "and in a way, he's right. When he lies down, there is more pulmonary congestion. That's his big problem now. After sitting up a few hours, he feels less congestion, so he sleeps again. Also, there may be less anxiety during the day."

The symptoms often accompanied the advanced stages of emphysema, and it had a name: orthopnea. It was a mean symptom. It left Frank exhausted much of the time; and since I often sat up with him and supported him while he dozed, it tired me, too.

Sometimes I was tired and heroic, and sometimes I was tired and horrible:

> May 11
> Came home from work to find Frank in bed and depressed. I felt really guilty. He says I complain all the time. He says he sees no hope, nothing to go on for.

I was tired and I couldn't take it. In the course of the evening, as I can put it together, I got his dinner and we watched some TV. I drank a lot. I remember saying, "Goddamn, Goddamn," as I did the dishes, and then going outside to cry. I remember telling him he hadn't showered in almost a week, and that I could cheerfully put a bullet in each of us that moment. And then I kicked that bedspread his mother had made down the stairs.

I am really some swell lady when I get into depression and alcohol. Frank took a shower and tried to cheer me. I don't know why I am so awful. I told him I was angry at the world, angry at God, for this. I said, "I finally found a man I can love, and our time together is so short." I am so angry at him for getting sick and leaving me.

In explosions like this, I finally began to see—and to admit to myself—that alcohol was an increasingly important factor. For some months I had been aware that my plan to use alcohol "to numb the pain a little" had gone wrong. I knew I was drinking too much—exactly how much I wasn't sure; I refused to keep track. I knew, though, that I had begun patronizing a second liquor store so that I wouldn't have to buy so much from one place.

I also had stopped drinking at lunch. That is not the good sign that it seems to be. It simply meant that, since one was not enough, I preferred not to start at all. Dimly, in the back of my mind, an alarm was sounding, but I silenced it by telling myself that if I was really in trouble with alcohol, Frank would know it and tell me.

Like me, Frank was dimly aware of the problem; and, like me, he didn't want to face it. Then one evening I made such a hash of everything—dinner burned, telephone messages scrambled, important papers mislaid—that my actions simply called out for explanation. Frank gave me a quizzical look: "What's gotten into you?"

I sat down at the kitchen table and, with a great sense of relief, got it out: "Do you have any idea how much I've been drinking lately?"

"I thought the Scotch bottle was going down awfully fast these days."

"I don't understand it. For thirty years I drank moderately. And now I just can't control it. After I've had enough, I see my hand reach out and pour another one. I don't want to do it, but I do it, anyway."

"Darling, that's what alcoholism is."

"What?"

"Losing control. Having more than you intended to have. Not being in charge of it anymore."

"I'm an alcoholic, then?"

"You're in the early stages, but that's what it is."

"I never thought it could happen to me."

"I didn't think so, either. I don't know when you crossed over the line, but you're addicted to it now. You can never safely drink again. And you will save yourself an awful lot of trouble and suffering if you just quit now—before it interferes with your health or your job."

He had confirmed what I already guessed. I put the Scotch bottle away; and while Frank was alive, I never had another drink.

It was not as hard to do as I thought it would be. I knew I had to quit—for Frank's sake and for my own. I had stopped thinking of alcohol as helping me cope with my problems. Clearly it was creating problems of its own; and it seemed to me that if I was going to get through what lay ahead, I did not need any extra burdens.

I realized that one more thing had gone wrong, but I was beyond the point where it mattered. Besides, on the scale of trouble as I knew it then, this looked small and unimportant. It was almost a relief to have a problem that I could do something about.

It pleased Frank immensely when I quit, and it brought us closer together. He felt good that he had helped me identify alcoholism in its early stages. "You've spared yourself an awful lot of trouble in the future," he said.

Chapter 12
Break, Break, Break

> Break, Break, Break
> At the foot of thy crags, O Sea!
> But the tender grace of a day that is dead
> Will never come back to me.
> Alfred, Lord Tennyson, *Break, Break, Break*

"If you took in only the amount of oxygen that he is getting," a doctor told me, "you would be unconscious in five minutes."

"How does he manage, then?"

"His body has become accustomed to it."

In the last four months of Frank's life, the oxygen level in his blood was always so low that any emergency room would have admitted him to the hospital at any time. He operated on a thin margin, and someone had to be with him all the time to watch that margin and decide when a man who was always terribly ill had become worse.

I watched for the tell-tale signs of low oxygen—the blue fingertips and grey face, the forgetfulness, the drowsiness, and finally the inability to comprehend exactly what was going on.

When these symptoms started showing, we tried to head them off. Sometimes we turned up the dial on the "walker" to increase the amount of oxygen that he breathed. Sometimes Frank increased the dosage of some medication, usually prednisone. In his struggle to keep going, he used the nebulizer recklessly, spraying an adrenalin-based broncho-dilator into his throat whenever he felt the need. Where once he had used it four or five times a day, he now used it that many times each hour. And constantly we worked with the available machines—dehumidifers, air conditioners, fans—to get the right temperature and humidity.

Frank hated hospitals, and I always delayed as long as I could. Eventually he became disoriented; then while he could still walk and was still aware enough to his condition to agree that he needed help, I took him to the hospital.

I did it often enough to develop a routine: Call the doctor. Find out if he can meet us at the hospital, or, if not, who I should look for. Get the "hospital bag," already packed with pajamas, robe, toothbrush, and books. Take all his medicines in case the doctors want to know what he's taking. Make sure you have the hospitalization card. Toss a paperback book and a packet of crackers in your purse. Pull the car up to the door and get the air conditioner going. Help Frank in.

Park in front of the emergency room. Run inside for a wheelchair. Come back and argue with the cop who enforces parking regulations.

"You can't leave the car there."

"I have to. There's no other place to park. I'm taking my husband into the emergency room."

"This area is only for stopping, not for parking. You should have someone with you to drop you off."

"Well, I haven't got anyone with me."

"We may have to tow the car away."

"Please don't," I said the first three times.

For the last hospitalization, though, I refused to be hassled. "Listen," I said. "I'm a personal friend of the county executive, Larry Hogan. You move this car one inch, and I'll have Larry on the phone so fast it will make your head spin. You'll lose your badge."

"All right. Move it as soon as you can."

Push the wheelchair inside.

It was fast after that. In minutes Frank always had three or four doctors and nurses working on him.

Stay near and answer questions. Keep the bag with the medications with you in case they ask about them. When you see that you're not needed, go to the admissions desk and register. Then park the car in the garage.

Come back and find Frank. If he's not still in the emergency room, he will be either in a room or in intensive care.

Intensive care. You can't go in. Call and let them know you're here. Find out what you can. Get the name of the doctor in charge of his case. Ask when you can call again.

Wait.

Wait.

Hope. Come on, Frank. You have pulled through this before. You can do it again. You can make it.

One of these times Frank isn't going to make it. The doctor is going to come through that door and say, "I'm sorry, Mrs. Sartwell. We did everything we could, but we just couldn't pull him through. This illness puts a great strain on the heart. In the end, his failed."

Do I want that to happen? Is that what I'm hoping for? Do I want this to be the end?

Of course, not.

Well, maybe. The end is coming. It's coming soon. Why not now? Now—before he suffers any more. Now—while I'm still all right. Now—while the memories, or most of them, are good. Now—before I really want it to happen. Yes, now. Let it be now.

No, I must not think like that. When Frank dies, I won't have him anymore. Not ever. And that's going to be worse.

Don't think about it. Don't think about anything. Find something to read.

Wait.

Four times Frank was in intensive care, and four times he recovered enough to go into a regular room for two or three weeks and then home.

The new enemy was edema. Not only did it cause his ankles and legs to swell so severely that he sometimes could not wear socks, but it also added to the strain on his heart. He had two medicines now that were vital to him—prednisone for his lungs and digoxin for his heart.

During one hospitalization, Frank was moved from intensive care to a room, and for several days he made good progress. Then, suddenly, he became so weak and ill that everyone thought he would die. I told all of our sons to visit soon.

When Cris and Adam, now 21 and 19, visited, Frank tried to talk, but he didn't have the breath to do it. They spent half an hour trying to buck up his spirits and putting a brave face on their own feelings. Then these two young men, who still spent much of their time together pummeling and insulting one another, walked sadly down the hospital corridor with their arms around each other's shoulders. They had already lost him once; now they were losing him again.

Dan, home for a brief visit after graduating from college, brought his guitar. Since Frank could hardly talk and Dan didn't know what to say, he hoped Frank would like to hear him play.

"I thought I'd mash down the guitar strings for you, Frank," said Dan, repeating Frank's favorite way of describing what Dan did to a guitar.

"I'd like that," Frank whispered.

As the strains of Bach's *Bouree in E Minor* filled the room with its sense of order and harmony, Frank lay back against the pillows. The other patient in the room and his relatives finished their conversation and listened. A few nurses came and stood in the doorway. Then he played Dvorak's *Danza* and finally Ravel's poignant *Pavonne pour les Infanta Difunte*. For fifteen minutes, in the midst of illness and pain, music created an oasis of beauty and sweetness. Then Dan put the guitar in its case, took Frank's hand, and choked out a goodbye.

Later that afternoon we discovered why Frank had taken such a sudden turn for the worse.

"How much prednisone is he getting?" I inquired of a nurse.

"Oh," she said, "he isn't getting any prednisone at all."

"How can that be? He's been taking high doses of that for almost three years. They can't just take it away suddenly. That could kill him."

It turned out that he hadn't been getting digoxin, either. A nurse, in transferring his medications from one chart to another, had copied everything on the front of the card but had neglected to flip the card over and copy the medications on the back.

I felt a surge of fury toward the nurse and at my own powerlessness to control what happened to Frank in the hospital. One minute dedicated doctors and miraculous machines saved his life, and the next minute an inattentive nurse endangered it. It was the same kind of wild contradiction that I experienced with the emergency room: to get to its breathtaking efficiency, you first had to get past the cop who hassled you about parking. You never knew which part of the system you were going to hook into at any given time, but you had no choice except to go ahead and use the system anyway.

After a week or more, the level of oxygen in his blood would rise to a certain level, the edema would diminish, and Frank would come home. In two or three weeks he would start to decline, and I would begin the countdown for the next hospitalization. I wondered how long we could go on this way.

> July 17
> Frank sits on the edge of the bed, falling forward as he goes to sleep, then rousing himself. Goes, "Oh," in pain, gasping. Nothing I can do.
>
> This can only get worse—more hospitalizations, then nurses, home care, bedpans. He can't work much longer. Mind not working well. Not always clear-headed when we talk.

Worried about me, too: How long can I go on? What if I get sick? What if I can't control my despair? Will I do something desperate and hate myself the rest of my life for it?

July 25
Marc says I must try to detach myself emotionally from Frank. Says it will be better for me and better for Frank. I try to do that—to be just the unemotional, dependable person who prepares low-sodium meals and fills oxygen tanks. But it's hard to stay detached from someone you have loved and whom you still love.

In July, over Frank's protests, I converted the downstairs den into a bedroom for him. The protests were purely for face-saving purposes; he was glad he wouldn't have to struggle up the steps anymore. Still, I knew he regarded the move as one more defeat, and I tried to soften it as much as possible. I did not want it to look like a makeshift room for an invalid. So Cris and Adam helped bring down not only a bed and chest of drawers but a desk and all the bookcases and books that the room could accommodate. With our Chincoteague photos against the wood paneling, the room looked more like a study than a bedroom. I was quite pleased with what had been accomplished. Frank tried to show pleasure, too, but it was a permanent reminder that he was losing the battle. His morale sagged, and he could not conceal it. His reaction disappointed me, and I could not conceal that. Sometimes the illness so distorted everything, even the best intentions, that it was impossible to avoid wounding one another.

I dared not look ahead. I had already given, it seemed to me, all my energy and love, and they had not really been enough. What was coming was bound to be worse, and I had nothing more to give. Frank's words, "We Sartwells do not abandon our wounded," ran through my mind all the time. I knew I had to see him through somehow. I would do it well if I could. If I couldn't do it well, I would do it somehow.

It began to go through my mind, though, that "seeing Frank through" was all I really had to do. I had no obligations after that. Dan had graduated and was on the road playing with a group called "The East Coast Brass." He didn't need me. Cris and Adam didn't need me, either. Cris planned to go to graduate school and get a degree in philosophy. ("Why philosophy?" Frank asked. "Sheer greed," Cris replied.) Adam was doing well, finishing his sophomore year at the University of Maryland and working part-time for NASA. Thanks to my new boss and a loyal staff, my job was pleasant again, but nothing that could be construed as a purpose in life. I had to face Frank's slow decline and eventual death, and I had to do my best to see him through. But I decided I could stop worrying about how I would go on after Frank died because there was no pressing reason for me to go on. It didn't matter, then, that I was physically exhausted and emotionally frayed. All I needed was enough to make it through this last long haul.

In late July Frank went back into the hospital for a couple of weeks. The hospitalization broke his decline and gave him, temporarily, a little boost of energy. A few days after he came home, we had a weekend when the usually hot, humid Washington weather suddenly turned benevolent. For a few hours the illness receded into the background.

"Let's go down to the Smithsonian," Frank suggested, "and see the peregrines."

"I didn't know there were peregrines there. Do you mean stuffed ones?"

"No, live ones. Young ones. They've got a joint program with Cornell University to bring back the peregrines. Cornell gets the eggs and hatches them. When the birds are old enough, they're placed in a roosting box on top of the Smithsonian and fed there. But they are free to fly. The idea is that while they are dining at the Smithsonian's expense, they are supposed to be learning how to find their own dinners. It's called 'hacking back.'"

We drove to the Castle, oldest of the Smithsonian buildings, and sat for a while in the Victorian garden there, admiring the roses and patterned hedges and enjoying the scent of thyme on the warm breeze.

Frank amazed me by walking half-way around the building and then about fifty feet away from it so that he could see the roosting box on the top. He was amused to see that some light-hearted ornithologist had painted battlements on the box to match those on the Castle. And when he saw two of the slate-backed peregrines swoop into the box, he was elated.

He came home and wrote a column joining the debate on whether men should take an endangered species from the wild and attempt to save it from extinction. Not surprisingly, he thought it was worth going to great lengths to preserve a species, and he made the case eloquently:

> Too much has happened; we have made the planet so much our own that little flies here without our concurrence, deliberate or unthinking. We had best stand ready to lay hands on a species, if that's what it takes, and protect it, husband it, re-create it if we must, and release it when we can, to stitch together the rents in our own planetary layer of life.

It was his last editorial. And those hours at the Smithsonian were almost the last good ones. One more good afternoon together was all that we were to have, but the memory of that would sustain me for a long, long time.

Chapter 13
Butterflies Are Forever

> It is eternity now. I am in the midst of it.
> It is about me in the sunshine; I am in it,
> As the butterfly in the light-laden air.
> Richard Jeffries, *The Story of My Heart*

There is a certain look on the face of someone who is close to death. I had seen it on the face of my 79-year-old aunt when her heart began to wear out and on the face of a friend, stricken early in life with cancer. It is a drawn look, and the eyes seem to focus on something not in this world. Frank had that look now.

If dreams are a key to our unconscious, then perhaps at that level Frank knew that he was dying and accepted it. For he dreamed one night that his father was on an island; and when Frank took a bridge out to the island, his father got up from the desk where he had been writing, put his arm around Frank, and said, "Well, son, I just didn't have time to finish it." I asked Frank what he thought that meant.

"My father wasn't editor of *Defenders*," he said. "I guess I feel I've completed my father's work."

The struggle with illness now dominated every day and virtually every hour. Frank needed a lot in the final weeks.

"I am completely dependent on you," he said. "My life depends on you."

"I won't let you down, Frank," I told him.

I think it is fair to say that I did not. I always managed to be there when he needed me and to do what needed to be done. Much of the time I did it with love and good humor. But sometimes I let him see that he was a burden and that I felt he was ruining my life. For I wanted it to be over—wanted it sometimes with a desperation that I could not always conceal.

We had arrived at the place toward which we had been heading for more than two years. Bit by bit the illness had taken over our lives, and bit by bit it had used up our physical and emotional reserves. I saw a life ahead with nothing in it except a hopeless illness, and I realized suddenly that I had never planned on facing it.

In the back of my mind, I had clung to the belief that I would not have to face a long, terrible ending—months or years of having a bedridden husband whose mind did not work well. A friend had once said to me, "Frank will never do that to you. At a certain point he will just take himself out of it."

I didn't want to put too precise a meaning on "take himself out of it." I simply filed the words away and took comfort in thinking that I would be spared the worst. I would loyally stick with Frank through his long decline, and then when we hit bottom—when life had nothing in it except a hopeless struggle against illness—Frank would "take himself out." Presumably by dying of natural causes when that time had come. But I also thought that there were circumstances in which I would commit suicide; and though we had never discussed it, I assumed that Frank shared my views.

Then one day we did talk about suicide, and I learned that Frank did not share my views at all. He wanted all of life that he could have, regardless of the quality. "It isn't much of a life, but it's the only life I've got," he said, "and I want to live it."

It does me no credit, but it is part of the record that my first reaction was to be jolted by what this might mean for *me*. I could no longer dismiss the stories of emphysema patients who spent five years bedridden as something I would never have to face.

There is nothing to be proud of in my feelings at the time. One consolation is that I concealed them well enough so that Frank did not know how I felt. Another is that the only thing I did about my feelings was to write them down:

Sunday, August 23
Frank just came out of the hospital two weeks ago. Shows many signs of needing it again.

I always thought when no good days were left, he would call off the struggle. Not so. He wants to fight always. I let him know that he is a burden, that my life is hell.

He wants to go on, doesn't care if my life is hell, doesn't care what it does to me. He lived self-destructively all his life; now that there are no good days ahead, he wants to hang on. Never asked me if I want him to hang on or how I feel about helping him hang on. I am ashamed of how I feel, but he is taking everything from me. Love is gone, patience is gone, even sadness is gone. All I want is for it to be over. I am willing to do almost anything to get it over——kill him with an overdose of medicine, kill myself.

I feel driven to do terrible things, and I am angry that I've been pushed so far. It isn't fair. I've taken so much and gone through so much, and I am not even going to be able to respect myself for that. I'm going to be pushed to violence and end up not even with a decent and respectable grief. I won't even have bearable memories.

I never agreed to this. I never consented to give everything to help keep someone's body alive. It's destroying everything. He's a very destructive man in his witty Irish way.

I have no acceptable alternatives. I can make a slave of myself to his illness, which is what he wants, and pretend to admire his strength of will in going on—now that every day is hell for him and hell for me.

I don't think I can go on.

I think I must kill either Frank or me. Or both of us. He is determined to go on this way. I am determined not to.

Later in the day I added this to the journal:

I have to try to look at this another way. I have to try to see Frank's side. Surely he has the right to die in a way that seems right for him. Suicide is probably against his principles. I think he is a Catholic at heart. His father lingered for two years; Frank can probably accept that and not feel that it's undignified.

I feel I am behaving with unbelievable selfishness expecting Frank to drop dead because he is a burden. And it's cruel to act out my resentment by being sullen and gloomy. I have to get these feelings under control.

In getting these feelings under control, it helped immensely to have a therapist. Nothing I said ever shocked Marc. So I told him how I longed for the end. I told him Frank was not going to end it. And I told him that I could not get the idea out of my mind that if I really couldn't stand any more, I could always end it myself. I told him I was becoming obsessed with the idea of killing Frank and then myself.

"I'm not surprised that you're thinking about it," Marc said calmly, "but I don't think you're capable of carrying it out. You think you could kill Frank because you see him suffering; but when it came right down to it, I don't believe you could do it. And I hope you don't because I know darned well you couldn't live with it. As for suicide, you think now that you don't want to go on after Frank dies. I think you will go on. I think you're a survivor. Listen to me, Marcia. I want you to survive."

Writing it out and talking it out helped. My obsession with murder and suicide abated. Not that the idea never went through my mind again. It did. But I had looked at it and rejected it; when it came back, it has less force. The next time suicide came up, I handled it better.

> Monday Sept. 2
> Labor Day weekend was a hard one. Frank seemed in need of hospitalization on Saturday—heavy, glazed eyes, falling asleep sitting up, mind not good. He couldn't remember what bills he had paid or what he had done with one of his checkbooks. I tried to help him remember, and I'm not sure he understood my questions because he gave such contradictory answers. At one point I said, 'Frank, that's no answer.' And in an almost childlike way, he said, 'It is an answer, it is, it is.'
>
> He said he was thinking about suicide: 'Why stay around waiting for everything to turn sour?'
>
> I told him I didn't want him to do it.

I am trying to figure my degree of guilt in those feelings. I am not the cheerful, always hopeful person he wants me to be. But I keep most of my bleak outlook to myself.

And he is finally getting some feelings out, too. The last few nights he has had anxiety attacks, and they make him so short of breath that it is terrifying for both of us. I tell him to start talking, to talk about whatever is on his mind. He pours out old guilts and resentments and anger, and it helps. In a few minutes he breathes all right again. He has poured out some amazing stuff from way back in his childhood. Who would think that when his mother told him he must try to be more like his cousin Jerry, he would carry that sense of her disappointment in him all his life, and forty years later the anger and hurt over that are still so intense they choke off his breath?

He says he literally cannot live without me, and he wants me to help him go on. I will. I am surprised how much love seems to be there still.

Sept. 5
Took Frank to the hospital on Tuesday, Sept. 3. All day Tuesday at work I had a premonition of trouble, so I left work early and got home to find him sitting in the dining room looking out of the window and waiting for me to come home. He had forgotten how to use the telephone, and he had no breath to do it, anyway. But he knew when I came home he would see me first through the dining room window. 'I knew you would know what to do,' he said. I helped him dress and took him to the hospital.

Dr. Steinberg met us there and got Frank into intensive care again. Then he came over to talk with me.

'I think he's going to make it,' he said. 'He's responding to treatment. Do you have any questions you want to ask?'

'I don't have any questions about the treatment or the outlook. The only question I have is how long this will go on, and you don't have the answer to that.'

'No.'

Steinberg wanted to know how I was holding up, and I said I didn't think I could go on taking care of Frank alone any more. He thinks the time has come to look for some help and will keep him in the hospital till I can find a practical nurse or something.

Sept. 9
Frank called me at work today and said that he is feeling better and looking forward to going home. I told him that I needed to find some home nursing care for him before I brought him home. He said he felt rebuffed—as if the worst thing in the world would be to get well and come home.

I said, 'No, Frank, the best thing in the world would be to get well and come home, but we both know. . .'

'I've had enough of reality,' he said.

Marc says I am at the end of my rope, and, indeed, I feel it. I can't take much more—can barely face what it means to have him home again—awake all night, sleeping all day, unshaven, mind unclear, temper testy, demanding good cheer. He is like a drowning man clutching a life preserver, and I feel myself going under.

Sept. 13
This should not be just a record of distress, anger, and despair. Even though some of the memories are bad—taking him to the hospital last time, seeing him in such awful condition was bad—but now a week later, I remember the good things. I feel my love for him.
I want to be with him again, I think I can take the bad days, and I look forward to some good ones.

I decided not to put Frank in a nursing home or a hospice but to go with the simplest solution and get someone to stay with him during the day. I thought of Laurie, a kind young woman who had worked for us as a house cleaner. I explained the situation to her and asked if she wanted the job.

"I don't know much about taking care of sick people," she said, "but I love Mr. Sartwell, and I really want to help."

"You'll do," I said.

Frank was desperately eager to get out of the hospital. He wanted to come home. And he wanted me to take him, as soon as possible, to Chincoteague.

"Okay," I said, trying to conceal my misgivings.

He saw them. "We're playing with the house money," he said.

The doctors were giving up. Nothing was working very well. Frank's legs were swollen up to the knee with edema, despite massive doses of a diuretic. I told Dr. Steinberg that I had found help and would take Frank home if he would discharge him.

"We're not doing him much good here," he said. "When does your lady start to work?"

"Not for a week and a half. But I want to take him home before that. He wants to go to Chincoteague."

"Okay, if you're willing to try it. Why don't you take him home on Sunday? That will give him a couple more days here."

On Saturday afternoon when I visited him in his eighth-floor room, Frank had an air of excitement about him.

"I'm a very lucky man," he told me.

"You certainly are," I said, taking what I thought was a cue for game-playing, "a beautiful wife, handsome and intelligent sons, an adoring stepson. . ."

"No, I mean it. You know what I've been doing today?"

"No."

"I have been lying in bed watching the butterflies migrate. Other people are lying in bed listening to the nurses bang bedpans or the patients complain. I am watching butterflies migrate. I'm lucky to have that kind of a mind."

"I didn't know butterflies migrated."

"Most people don't. All the monarch butterflies on the East Coast are headed for two trees in Pacific Grove in California. Thousands of butterflies cling to those two trees in the winter, and the trees are so thick with butterflies that you can hardly see the green branches. I think that's a miracle. How do these butterflies, which were hatched here from larvae, know which two trees in California they want? And where do they stow their navigational gear?"

I took this photo very early in our relationship, before butterflies became so symbolic to us.

He caught me up in the wonder of it. And he was right. Every five minutes or so a monarch butterfly went by, heading west. All afternoon I sat on the bed with him, and we held hands, and together we watched the miracle of the butterflies.

"I'm a very lucky woman," I said when I kissed him goodbye. I meant it.

Chapter 14
A Narrow Time

> We waited while she passed;
> It was a narrow time,
> Too jostled were our souls to speak. . .
> — Emily Dickinson, *The Last Night*

On Sunday Frank came home from the hospital, and on Tuesday I packed up the car with clothes for a week, the 65-pound "cow" newly filled with oxygen, and all our camera equipment. I thought the possibility of our taking photos was pretty remote, but Frank did not agree.

"Do you think you'll need the tripod, Frank?"

"Better take it along."

"And the 40 mm lens?"

"Might be nice to have it."

But it was a terrible trip, and what little optimism we started with disappeared before we were half-way there. Twenty-five miles outside of Chincoteague Frank suddenly was seized with pain in his stomach. "Oh. . .oh. . .oh," he cried out.

"What do you need?" I shouted. "A toilet?"

He thought so. But when I found a gas station, I knew I couldn't get him into the rest room alone. I was about to go for help when the pain subsided. There was no way he could even tell where he hurt or what he needed. We drove on, and we made it.

He wanted to go out to his favorite restaurant for dinner, or at least he thought he did. When we got there he ordered all his favorite dishes, but he could not eat. I realized it had been a terrible mistake to come, and I decided to try to persuade him to go home the next day.

That night I woke, restless, and went to Frank's bedroom. He was not there. I found him sitting at the picnic table on the porch and trying to hold himself upright. The night was damp and foggy—the worst possible weather for him, but I realized that didn't really make a difference anymore. I put a blanket over his shoulders and supported him for a few hours while he dozed. Toward dawn he went back to bed, and, overcome with weariness, I slept, too.

When I woke Wednesday morning, I told him we should go home. He understood why, but it was a final defeat for him. He knew he would never be back.

We sat on the front porch for awhile before leaving, each of us in a mood of black despair. Suddenly, a bird landed on the porch, and for an instant Frank brightened. "Look," he said, "a warbler!"

I was too depressed even to turn and look. It was my last chance to share with Frank his delight in birds, and I missed it.

I did, though, get us packed and back to Washington safely. I called Laurie when we got home, and she said she could start work the next day.

"Come around 8 o'clock, and I'll go over the medicines with you and show you how to fill the portable oxygen tank," I said.

I stayed with Laurie until 10 the next morning, making out charts for the times of Frank's medications and writing down everything I thought she might need to know.

I could see that Frank was not good at all, and I was uneasy about leaving. But what was the point in hiring someone to look after him while I worked if I didn't go to work? Finally, I left.

At noon the phone call came. "I'm sorry for calling you at work, Mrs. Sartwell, but Mr. Sartwell is acting very strange, and I just don't know what to do."

"I'll be right home, Laurie."

He was ashen grey and incoherent. The edema had never been so bad. I called the doctor and described his symptoms.

"When was Frank in the hospital last?"

"Sunday. Four days ago."

"There's nothing we can do anymore. I'm sorry, Mrs. Sartwell."

"Is he dying, then?"

"Yes. Do you want to bring him into the hospital, or do you want to keep him home?"

"I'd like to have him at home if that's possible."

"It's the most humane thing to do."

"What shall I do for him?"

"Keep him as comfortable as you can."

"How long do you think it will be?"

"Five or six hours. I'm sorry. We all have to go sometime."

This was it, then. This was not another emergency. It was the end. Death was coming. I thought I would feel something special but I seemed to have switched into a gear where I became very efficient but felt nothing at all.

I called Adam and told him it looked as if his father was dying.

The silence lasted a long time. Finally: "I guess I knew this phone call was coming soon." Then: "What hospital is he in?"

"No hospital. I'm going to keep him at home. The doctor agrees."

"Can you take care of him?"

"Yes, but I'd like you and Cris to come if you can."

"I'll get Cris, and we'll be right over."

Frank was sitting at the desk in the bedroom and struggling to stay upright. Even semi-conscious, he sensed that he was holding death at bay by keeping his heart and lungs high while the fluid gathered. I stacked pillows on the desk so that he could rest against them.

Cris and Adam arrived. They agreed that Frank would want to die at home. Then Frank said something, and Cris leaned forward to catch it.

"I didn't hear what he said, but if he's trying to talk, maybe there's hope," he said. "Maybe he should go to the hospital. Do you mind if I call the doctor?"

"No, I don't mind. I want you to feel all right about it."

"You're right," he said a few minutes later, "but I had to know."

"Frank," I said, "Cris and Adam are here."

He understood, and it pleased him. He tried to understand what was happening. "How did I get here?" he asked.

"You're not in the hospital. You're home. We're going to take care of you here."

He smiled. "You're so good to me."

He talked very little after that, and there wasn't much we could do for him except sit beside him and support him, wipe the perspiration from his face with a cool cloth, offer water. Once he spoke to Cris. "It's hard," he said, "it's hard to let go."

The hours went by. Adam went out to McDonalds and brought back some hamburgers.

"It's just like Dad to be a whole lot tougher than anyone expected," Adam said.

"He always said he would 'not go gentle,'" said Cris.

The phone rang. It was my next door neighbor, who was calling from her son's home, an hour's drive away. She hoped she had remembered to leave the porch light on for her return. If not, would I mind letting myself in her house and turning on the light?

In a voice that sounded strangely matter-of-fact, I said I'd be glad to, and I went out the back door and into the yard. The light was on. Everything was just as it always was, the houses solid and comfortable, the porch light illuminating the driveway and the lilac bushes beside it, the night peaceful. It seemed incredible to me that inside my home a drama of pain and loss was taking place, and the universe was taking no notice.

Back in Frank's room, Cris and Adam had moved him to the bed, but he did not want to lie down. It became more difficult to hold him up now because his arms flailed about and he was a dead weight, but clearly he wanted to remain sitting up.

"There's no use in all of us staying up all night," I said. "Let's divide the night into watches, and each of us take one. I'll stay with him from 11 to 2 a.m. Cris, would you take from 2 to 5, and Adam from 5 o'clock on. If there is any change, whoever is with him should wake everyone else."

I was not far into my watch when I realized that I had a very sore throat and was getting a cold—my first in three years. It was strange that I should come down with a cold almost on the very hour I could stop worrying about the consequences of passing it on to Frank. I thought a little Scotch would make my throat feel better. And whether or not I drank no longer mattered now. Nothing mattered now, or ever would again.

I found that it worked better to hold Frank with both arms encircling him. It kept him from falling forward and it restrained his arms. I wrapped both arms around him in a tight embrace and held on. Two hours passed.

Cris came down at 1 o'clock. "I couldn't sleep anymore," he said. "Do you need any help?"

"No, I'm fine, but I'm glad to have you here."

Cris sat down on Frank's right side and helped support him.

Suddenly Frank sat up straight and opened his eyes. He looked straight ahead at, or through, the window. Cris and I followed his gaze. I saw nothing but the dark night, with a little reflection of the lamp on Frank's bedside table. Frank never took his eyes away from the window, but remained focused and serious. He had an air of anticipation, as if he were about to be given an award or honor. Intent, it seemed, on presenting a more dignified appearance, he adjusted the collar of his pajamas and smoothed his beard. Then he ripped off the cannula and threw it scornfully aside. He sat erect and alert for a few more seconds, and then, breathing a deep sigh, he slumped again. Cris and I lowered his head to the pillow and swung his feet onto the bed. He was in a deep coma.

"He threw that cannula aside as if he knew he'd never need it again," I said to Cris.

"I know. And he looked as if he were—well, arraying himself, or something."

"Cris, when you looked out the window where he was looking, did you see anything?"

"No," he said, "but Dad did."

We sat for a moment together. "I don't understand it," he said.

"Neither do I." But I will never forget it. Something just happened. I don't know what it was, and I can't think about it now. But I will think about it someday.

After a moment, looking at Frank's still form, Cris said, "Why don't you get some sleep? There's no need for both of us to be here."

I went out into the kitchen and my eyes fell on the calendar. It was early in the morning of September 26—exactly six years from the day I had first told Frank of my love for him.

I slept till 4 a.m., when I heard Frank cry out. I dashed downstairs to him, but he lay perfectly still. "What happened?" I asked Cris.

"I don't know." Then: "Marcia, I think he's dead."

From the stony look in Frank's eyes, I thought that Cris was right, but I checked for a pulse or sign of breathing. Nothing.

Then I closed his eyes and kissed his forehead. "Good night, Frank."

No tears came that day. I moved through it with robot-like efficiency, all the while watching myself from a distant spot on the ceiling, where I felt I was floating. The doctor had told me that when a person dies at home, the first thing you must do is notify the state police because Maryland law requires it. So, shortly after 5 a.m. we had a burly state trooper wearing a gun, poking around and asking questions. I answered all of them quite patiently, and after nearly an hour, he phoned his office to report that the man had died "apparently of natural causes," and he went away.

I called the crematorium, where I'd made previous arrangements, and told them Frank had died and that they should pick up his body. I watched him go, and later, just before the cremation, I went there to identify him. I thought he looked more like the Frank I had fallen in love with than the ill person he had become. "Yes, that's Frank," I said.,

Frank loved all the birds, especially hawks and egrets; he thought gulls were funny, survivors, beautiful fliers.

I arranged with Rev. Wofford Smith, our neighbor and a chaplain at the University of Maryland, to hold a memorial service at his chapel on campus. I called a friend who sang beautifully and asked her to take charge of the music. I asked a good friend to speak. Cris said he would like to read a poem. We drew up the program together. I gave Cris and Adam my credit card and told them to buy nice suits and some dress shoes for the service.

I called Frank's mother, who was recovering from surgery and unable to come to the service. She said Frank was always a Catholic in his heart and she wanted him buried as one. Later she asked other members of the family and a priest or two to call with the same request. Distressed though I was about the calls and her unhappiness, I didn't think she was right. And even if she were, there was no way the robot I had become would have known how to change course and do anything but carry out the plans already in place.

I called people, and people called me. One "friend" of Frank's called to say he was sorry he hadn't seen Frank for so many months. "But," he said, "emphysema is a pretty easy way to die, isn't it?" Most calls were more consoling. People liked Frank; they would miss him, too.

I talked with the obit writer from *The Washington Post*, answered his questions, and put a picture in the mail for him. I talked with Frank's associate editor from *Defenders*, who was also writing a piece about him.

Dan arranged to get two days off, and I picked him up at the airport.

And then the memorial service: the beautiful end-of-September day, the filled chapel, Wofford's tribute to Frank's love of nature and love of life, beautiful music, Cris's defiant reading of Dylan Thomas's "Do Not Go Gentle," all tape-recorded for Frank's mother.

And still there were no tears. They gave me a box with his ashes. In addition to being an Episcopal priest, Wofford was a pilot. We flew from Washington to the Chesapeake Bay in a two-seater plane that he owned. When we were well out over the Bay, Wofford said some words, opened the window, and scattered the ashes.

My boss called me and told me to take all the time off I needed and not to come back to work until I felt better. I didn't think I would ever feel better, so I went back the next week. I worked a full day, not wanting to admit to anyone that I couldn't get my mind to focus on anything and could barely comprehend what was going on.

After work, I took the elevator down to the parking garage, and there, alone in the car, with no one to hold up for and no one to go home to, I cried.

Epilogue

> A death blow is a life blow to some.
> Emily Dickinson,

Part One: Five Years Later

When Frank died, it seemed to me that my life had stopped—and that therefore everything in the world must surely stop, too. I could scarcely believe that the sun came up as usual, that stores and offices opened and people went to work, that ads still came addressed to Frank Sartwell ("We know a lover of the outdoors like yourself would appreciate the comfort of these hiking boots").

Sometimes the feelings of sadness, guilt, longing, and despair were almost overwhelming; and sometimes there were no feelings whatsoever, just a kind of numbness where I observed my body moving about doing familiar things. I could never tell whether I was making "progress." One day the sadness would lift a little, and the next day I'd feel washed overboard with no land in sight. Somewhere in a book I came upon two wise observations: recovering from grief will take longer than you expect, and you will not be the same afterwards.

Grieving is a solitary process, although it doesn't seem so at first. Like many widows, I discovered that there is an immediate outpouring of sympathy and support. For two or three weeks I was inundated with cards, letters, phone calls, and invitations to dinner. Then they stopped. Except for a few close friends, almost nobody made a second sympathetic gesture. I was surprised to find out how fast the world is finished with your grief—and how fast it expects you to be done with it, too. The message is: Take a couple of weeks to deal with it, then pull yourself together and go on as if nothing significant has happened.

I soon realized that my presence often made people uncomfortably aware of their own mortality. And some friends, despite the best intentions, simply could not be in the presence of so much raw pain. About three weeks after Frank died, Mary and Geoff, good friends for more than two decades, invited me to dinner at a Georgetown restaurant. I was looking forward to an honest talk, but when I got there, another couple, whom I barely knew, was also at the table. After the obligatory, "We're so sorry about your loss," conversation moved to safe topics—weather, children, movies—with much light banter intended to be cheerful and distracting. I tried to join in, to be light-hearted and pretend that nothing had happened, but it is an ordeal to do that when, in fact, your heart is broken. When it was over, I put the evening down to good intentions gone awry.

A few weeks later Mary and Geoff again invited me to dinner. To my surprise, we were joined by the same couple, and so we repeated the previous evening's superficialities. This time I realized that Mary couldn't take me as I was. I guessed that my grief must be almost palpable to her and that she didn't like the feel of it. My very presence was so unsettling to her that to be with me at all, she had to have a buffer between us. Perhaps I reminded her that one day she, too, could lose a beloved partner, or perhaps she lived so much in her own intellect that she could not tolerate intense emotion. At any rate, I understood that under the circumstances we could no longer be friends. I sent her a thank-you note and did not see or hear from her again for nine years.

I felt isolated. I feared that never again would there be a place for me in the mainstream. I would live forever on the fringes of society— the third person in the car or the seventh at dinner, always feeling like an outsider. With Frank gone, I had little physical contact with anyone, and the well-meant pats on the shoulder from friends scarcely replaced

Epilogue

Frank's warm bear hugs. Sometimes I felt that an invisible space surrounded me and that no one could break through it.

I experienced grief as physical pain. I felt that in the back of my throat I had a golf ball, which I tried constantly to swallow down, and between my ribs I occasionally got a pain that pierced like a knife. I also had the strange sensation that a piece of me was missing, blown away somewhere.

I operated much of the time in a fog. My voice sounded strange to me, as if I were under water. It was difficult to concentrate. Once I set out to purchase something on the third floor of a five-level department store. I stepped on the escalator, forgot to get off, and rode it all the way to the top. Annoyed at myself, I got on the down escalator and did the same thing again, riding it all the way to the basement. When I got on again, it took an enormous effort to remember to get off on the third floor and then to recall what I wanted to buy.

I managed on the job because I didn't pretend to be more on top of it than I was. For many months, I slogged through on automatic most of the time, relying on ingrained habits and familiar routines. Most of the time they were enough to get the job done adequately. When they were not, two wonderful senior staff members rescued me, tactfully nudging me in new directions: "Are you sure you want to do it that way? I was wondering if we might try. . ."

When the day was over, I took the elevator to the parking garage, got into my car, put my head on the steering wheel, and let the tears flow. There in the car, I didn't have to hold up any more. No one noticed me; no phones rang; no one could even hear my noisy sobs. I drove home on roads that were a watery blur.

Nothing really mattered. In the back of my mind was a thought that kept edging itself forward: "If it doesn't get any better, I can always . . ."

About three months after Frank died, I realized that the decision had been made. There was no reason to go on. I could end the heartache and the struggle. It would be a cop-out, I realized, a selfish thing to do, and a terrible legacy to leave one's son. But at least Dan was through college and on his own. One day perhaps he would understand and forgive. The immediate problem was that my financial affairs were not in good order. I would need to straighten them out and make a will so that I didn't leave a tangled financial mess to further burden Dan and my two stepsons. Every time the thought of suicide came up, I told myself, "Yes, but not now. My financial affairs are a mess." And every time I told myself to call a lawyer and make a will, I put it off. It was as if the healthy part of me was playing for time.

For months I stood at the edge of this abyss and looked down. All through the first winter, when I came home to a big, empty house, I promised myself that I didn't have to go on doing this much longer. The abyss became almost a real presence, a dangerous, darkly reassuring one.

And yet I kept on going. After six months, I noted in my journal: "I welcome the passage of time. It does make things hurt less. Or maybe it's just that, in going on, we prove to ourselves that we can go on. And there is some comfort in that."

Another source of comfort, though, was more dubious. As soon as I got home from work, I poured a couple ounces of Scotch over a few ice cubes. Sometimes I didn't even take off my coat before fixing the drink. Then I had a second drink while preparing dinner, something quick and easy—a hamburger, perhaps, or another frozen dinner. I had no interest in cooking and couldn't taste food any more. But the Scotch was another matter. I could feel it warming me to the core. To keep the glow going—and the sad feelings at bay—I would have another drink after dinner and another before going to bed. The nightcap, I told myself, was to help me sleep, even though it didn't.

Every so often, I would take an honest look at what I was doing and worry that it was excessive and self-destructive. Then I would stop—once for three weeks and several times for three days. Always, though,

Epilogue

I began again because I didn't really care how self-destructive it was if it just made me hurt a little bit less.

For ten months after Frank died, I maintained this pattern of on-and-off drinking. Then one day when I came home from work, I put a couple of ice cubes in a glass, took down the bottle of Scotch, and as I held the bottle over the glass, I froze for a moment. There was my hand clutching a bottle and my arm in the sleeve of the coat I was still wearing. I was barely in the door, and already I was preparing to lose another evening of my life to alcohol. A wave of disgust overwhelmed me. I'm never going to get my life together if I keep on drinking this way, I thought. I don't want to do this. I don't want to die like this. I poured the Scotch into the sink. I didn't know whether I was an alcoholic or whether the situation had turned me into an alcohol abuser, and it didn't matter. I looked up AA in the phone book, went to a meeting that night, and stopped drinking.

About this time, an old friend, Dody, came back into my life. We had been friends since high school and lived together in Philadelphia as we started our careers, I with the Curtis Publishing Company, and she with the American Friends Service Committee. Twenty years ago the Friends had sent her to Rome, and she had never really come back. She had fallen in love with Ruggiero, an engineer. With their four children, they lived in an apartment in Rome and spent summers and weekends in their villa in Umbria. Though we had kept in touch, we hadn't seen each other for years. Now, just a year after Frank died, a letter came insisting on a visit.

This trip with a dear friend, who was now steeped in Italian art and history, lifted my spirits almost at once. Dody knew the best hours for getting into the Sistine Chapel without a wait, where to eat cheaply and magnificently, how to maneuver the tiny Cinquecento up the narrow, winding roads of the hill towns, when to arrive at Orvieto, and which café to be sitting at when the setting sun turned the cathedral's west façade into a blaze of gold.

At the beginning of the trip I said, "I'm sort of hostile to religion. Let's not go in any churches." She gasped, "But that's where the art is!" I conceded the point. After while, to my surprise, I started to like being in churches or cathedrals. It wasn't just that they were full of art treasures; it was also that being in places that were so very old filled me with awe. On the island of Torcello, off the coast of Venice, there is a church dating back to 639. The mosaics have a direct, almost primitive force. As we stood on the ancient mosaic pavement, I was tremendously moved. For more than a thousand years, I thought, people have stood on this spot, on the very stones where I stand now, and felt much as I do now. And generations to come will be here, looking at the same mosaics, feeling the same emotions. I felt part of a continuum, connected to the past and future. A phrase from my church-going youth came to mind and made sense: *As it was in the beginning, is now and ever shall be, world without end.*

I came home in good spirits, with the memories of the warm colors of Italy—the ochre buildings with their burnt sienna rooftops against a clear blue sky—forever imprinted in my memory, and with a desire to see more of this interesting world.

The trip was not a magic ending to the period of mourning, though. I came home to the same empty house. Soon Italy's sunny September skies turned to Washington's grey November clouds. Before long, the holiday season—the second one since Frank had died, but the first one I would attempt to go through without an alcoholic crutch—loomed ahead.

I made it easily through Thanksgiving, which was never a very sentimental occasion for me since I always had some reservations about the Pilgrims. I also made it through Frank's birthday on November 28, which, fortunately, was a busy workday. The next holiday, though, was the real hurdle. Frank used to say in jest, "The Christmas season is at our throats again," only now it didn't seem funny. It was literally true.

Epilogue

The golf ball in my throat returned, as did the sharp pain between my ribs. Once, jostled in a crowd of Christmas shoppers, I even thought someone might have stabbed me, and I unbuttoned my coat just to make sure no one had.

I knew Christmas would not be easy, but I thought I had been doing well since the trip. I'd even told myself that perhaps the worst of the grieving process was over. So I was not prepared for how quickly the Christmas season had thrown me into heavy seas. Every day seemed to open old wounds and deepen my sense of isolation. I felt assaulted on every side—the incessant Christmas carols; the tinsel and trees and Santa Clauses in every store and on every street; the relentless advertising; the getting and spending; the forced cheeriness.

If I'd felt that everything about Christmas was cheap and phony, it might have been easier to ignore it. But I didn't. Christmas wasn't just "Rudolph the Red-Nosed Reindeer," plastic Santas, cotton snow, and false good cheer. It was also Handel's *Messiah* and Bach's *Christmas Oratorio* and, even for someone like me who didn't go to church, a symbol of hope and love.

Christmas was also memories. Even when you try not to remember too much, they come, like a strand of Christmas lights, linked together, each laden with emotion: Mother at her happiest, singing carols as she turned out an array of delicacies—homemade chocolate truffles, decorated sugar cookies shaped like Santas or trees, fruitcake, gingerbread, stuffed dates, roast beef and Yorkshire pudding; Aunt Pearl arriving from New York with bundles of beautifully wrapped packages. And the wonderful Christmases with Frank, who loved everything about the season—loved to give gifts, loved to get them, loved the music and the smell of Christmas trees, loved the whole "gear and tackle and trim" of the season. How happy we had been then!

So happy, in fact, that we had decided to end one perfect Christmas season with the most joyous event of all and get married on New Year's

Day. "Now," said Frank after the ceremony, "when the bells ring out, we will know they ring for us."

Now the bells rang out, all right. They rang and rang; you couldn't stop them. On every corner someone rang a damned bell to remind me how alone I was and how I missed him.

I told myself the Christmas season would soon be over. All this would end. It would end.

But it wasn't going to end soon enough. I came home on December 13 feeling that I could not go on. Christmas was nearly two weeks away and what would have been our fifth wedding anniversary was one week after that. Every day was more of an ordeal than the previous one, and I was utterly depleted: out of ideas for coping, out of reasons to keep going, out of energy, unable even to pull myself together to make a phone call. I couldn't talk to anyone about how I felt, not when everyone was either happy or having his own struggles with the season.

I knew then that I would take a drink; I'd do anything that might numb the pain. But it was not just a drink; it was a terrible defeat. I had not drunk anything alcoholic for five months. I had been struggling to build a new life and to inhabit it fully—not with a foggy head or numbed feelings. To drink was to admit that I couldn't do it, that I couldn't come back. I felt myself slipping into darkness, sucked down, and I had nothing left with which to resist it.

I was in my bedroom, on the floor in a dejected heap. Then I was on my knees. "Oh, God," I said. "I don't even believe in you, but if you're there, please help."

How to explain what happened? For, in a sense, nothing happened. There was no flash of insight, no visions, no voices. I simply stayed there for half an hour or more, and then I felt better. I made a phone call and went out to see friends.

Nonetheless, it was a transforming event. As I knelt on that bedroom floor, the slide into darkness stopped. I began to feel better—less desperate, then calmer, then peaceful. I was not aware that anything was happening to me; I was just grateful for the inner quiet. Then the feeling that I was hollow inside and drained of resources disappeared, and I began to feel strength and a love of life pouring in and filling the empty place.

It seemed to me then, and still seems, almost miraculous. I had hit a kind of bottom and instead of shattering, I felt life renewing itself in me. It was not a religious conversion; it was not a command to devote my life to good works. The experience did not give me any great intellectual insight into life or death, and it certainly gave me no theology. It was a great, incomprehensible, and mysterious gift. I'd been plucked out of a place of despair and put down in another, far better one. Though I had done nothing to deserve it, something utterly beyond my understanding and inexpressibly awesome had touched my life.

A feeling of wonder and of something close to joy carried me through Christmas and New Year's and well beyond. Over the years, the feeling has diminished, but it has never entirely left me. Nothing like it has ever happened again. Nevertheless, the experience is part of me, and I have some hope that if I should ever be in such great need in the future, it will come again.

It would be pleasant to report that when such a transcendent moment happens to you, you are automatically excused from having to work through all the phases of grief. Alas, not so. I was feeling much stronger as I began the new year, but I still had to go through the step-by-step process of overcoming grief.

One of the problems I needed to overcome was my guilt. I had been mentally retracing each time I felt I had let Frank down and chastising myself for it. An article in *The Washington Post* helped. "People are most strange," Henry Fairlie wrote. "They search into every nook and cranny of themselves for one speck of dust, rather than be satisfied with the shining reflections of their own decency." After reading that, whenever I started poking about for those "specks of dust," I stopped and reminded myself of the far greater number of times I had been a loving wife, quick to see what Frank needed and to supply it. While acknowledging that I had been far from perfect as a caregiver, I knew I had done the best I could.

I learned to live with the knowledge that under stress I could think absolutely awful thoughts and fantasize terrible deeds. Something good actually came out of knowing that: I became a great listener. Friends could tell me anything about what they felt or thought, and nothing shocked or even surprised me anymore. Nor did I judge them. We are responsible for what we do, I decided, but not for what we feel. There is no point in condemning feelings, our own or anybody else's. Perhaps the best thing we can do is just be honest with ourselves about them.

For consolation during these years, I often turned to music, art, and poetry. I went regularly to concerts and recitals, and I went alone, by choice. Music often brings tears to my eyes, and this was especially true in the years after Frank died. I found it easier to sit by myself and let the tears come and, afterwards, quietly mop up than to try to choke them back or worry about what a companion might think. I was generally alone also when I visited art museums because most people want to see quite a few pictures when they go to a gallery, and I wanted to get deeply absorbed in only a few. I spent a lot of time looking at a Rembrandt self-portrait in the National Museum. He looks out at the world with such sad eyes that I felt I had found someone who understood my grief and had himself experienced much worse.

Poetry, though, I often read with a friend, Joan, also a recent widow. Before going out to dinner, we would read a few poems by Millay, Donne, Keats, and others. We had so much of it memorized that at dinner we often kept on reciting it. We both thought that nothing surpassed the poetry of Edna St. Vincent Millay when it came to expressing sorrow and loss. I could start a poem:

> The first rose on my rose tree
> Budded, bloomed and shattered,

Epilogue

and Joan would complete the stanza with:

> During sad days when to me,
> Nothing mattered.

Joan was one of the few friends I had who either had experienced what I was going through or who had an instinctive understanding of it. The love and support of a few such friends can carry you through a lot.

For two years after Frank died, I continued to see my therapist, Marc. We talked for a long time about grief; as it lessened, we talked more about my life. I began to understand myself a little better, especially the anger that had always been part of me. Marc once said, "You've got reasons for your anger. You were an unwanted, unloved child who was constantly compared to the older brother your parents adored. Of course you were angry and dared not express it. But when you were a kid, you probably needed that anger and a certain amount of scrappiness just to survive. The question is: Do you need it now?"

I began to feel a certain sympathy for the child who had been so buffeted at home and had suppressed so much sadness and anger. When I softened a little in my judgment of myself, I could tell that the anger softened, too, and it was a wonderful feeling. I did not have to work so hard to keep the lid on the powder keg, and so I had more energy and more space inside for other feelings. Also, since there was less anger, there was less fear that it might erupt uncontrollably, so I could relax a bit and trust myself more. I liked the new, less-angry person that I was, and I began to be gentler with myself, which meant that I was gentler with others, too.

Some of the assumptions I'd always had about myself were not holding up, and I abandoned them. The first to go was my sense of myself as a very efficient, independent person capable of handling things alone. The truth was that I couldn't run the office without the help of the staff, nor could I get through major holidays without Dan. I needed the love and support of good friends, whose help I accepted even though I didn't have much to offer in return. The protective shell began to crack, and I let it happen, welcoming the greater openness and even the greater vulnerability.

One day as we talked about the stress of Frank's long illness, Marc surprised me by observing, "The experience was the gift."

I bristled a little. "How can you say that, Marc? The experience was pain and loss."

"And out of that has come growth."

By the end of the second year after Frank died, the intense pain of loss was, for the most part, gone. There will always be moments when something brings it back—a line from a poem we read together; an aria from his favorite opera, Menotti's *Amahl and the Night Visitors*; the salty smell of the ocean at low tide; a hawk circling above—and it is astonishing how close to the surface the grief is and how it seems as if it all happened yesterday. In the truest sense I never recovered from Frank's death any more than I recovered from a traumatic childhood. The experiences are part of who I am. By another measure, though, I had completed the journey through grief in four years. This was the length of time it took to lose the sensation that some part of me was missing and to feel once more like a complete person in a whole body.

Five years on, I have recovered from Frank's loss in so many ways, and yet his love and the grief I still feel have become part of me in ways I scarcely understand. Last summer I traveled to Italy to visit Dody once again. I planned the trip so that September 26, the day Frank died, would fall in the middle of it. With the confusion of crossing time zones and with no need to use a calendar, I intended that the date would come and go without my being aware of it. And, indeed, Dody and I got so busy catching up with each other's lives and traveling—Venice this time—that I was never quite sure what the date was. Then one morning when I woke up feeling so ill that I thought I had the flu, I thought to ask, "What day is it?" "September 26," Dody replied. My

Epilogue

unconscious mind remembered; in fact, my whole body remembered. The love and grief I experienced are now, I believe, a part of me, embedded in every muscle, sinew, and fiber of my being.

I have given away Frank's clothes, his cameras, and most of his books; and long ago I sold the house in Chincoteague because I knew I could never go there without him. I have parted with the tangible evidence of his life, but I have tried to keep the intangible things: his love of nature and beauty, his joy in living. The dying man who looked out his hospital window and marveled at the migration of the butterflies—this was the man who had loved me and said, "You have an enormous capacity to enjoy life. Let it grow." This is his legacy, and I want to honor it.

Part Two: Thirty Years Later

I am rather glad I didn't publish this memoir earlier, when the grief was new or even when, after five years, I was well on my way toward recovery from it. Now I can look back upon this period of my life and see what effect it has had over the course of a long lifetime. Now I can say with certainty what I could not possibly have known then: that it is possible to have something absolutely devastating happen to you, to survive it, and to build a fulfilling, even joyful, life.

Though I was terribly sad during my first few years as a widow, it is clear to me from this perspective that I have had an amazing journey back. Great changes have taken place in my inner world, in my personality, in my way of relating to others, in my outlook on life. Frank's observation: "You have an enormous capacity to enjoy life. Let it grow" now seems more like a prediction, or perhaps a benediction.

Some of these have been hard-earned changes. Frank's death stripped away so much—love, companionship, a way of life—that I was forced to change, to learn how to reach out and at the same time to find greater strength in myself. For a long time I felt that I had been broken; later,

I knew I was mending. In the breaking, I lost much of my brittleness, defensiveness, and arrogance. In the mending, I became gentler, more open to friendship, and more accepting of human frailties, including my own dark side that is so evident in this memoir.

I have discovered great joy in being alive. Each year has brought something new into my life. Who would ever think that one's sixties would be better than her fifties, or that the seventies would be better still? And yet for me each decade has been better than the one before. There has been an almost miraculous opening up to new experiences and to people, and at the same time there has been a turning inward—not a morbid turning in, but a greater calm and a sense of ease with myself and with solitude. The feeling of connectedness that came to me in Torcello has come many times now: on an excavated street in the city of Ephesus; in a cave on the island of Patmos in the Aegean Sea, where legend has it that St. John composed the Book of Revelations; and in less exotic settings—on the shore of the ocean, or in a concert hall while listening to Verdi's *Requiem*.

I know I am not the only person to experience this kind of rebirth after surviving a tragedy. Surely that was what Emily Dickinson was referring to when she said, "A death blow is a life blow to some," and what Hemingway had in mind when he wrote in *A Farewell to Arms*: "The world breaks everyone and afterward many are strong in the broken places." In *Transformations*, psychiatrist Roger Gould describes it this way: "Some of us awaken from this nightmare slide downhill and through a flash of insight and tremendous commitment of will initiate changes leading back to our true inner self. . . . Sometimes this occurs only after a severe loss, followed by a deep mourning reaction. The loss then becomes the source of an unintended and unexpected miracle: the men and women who came alive at the end of their lives."

Something like this has happened to me. I hesitate to call it a miracle, but if it is not a miracle, it will do until a real one comes along.

Epilogue

I did not need to find another life partner to do this. I had not been looking for a partner when I met Frank, but I loved him almost immediately. After he died, I neither looked for a new partner nor ruled out the possibility of finding one. It simply did not happen.

I did not do this alone, though. I had the support of friends and family, the gift of good health and a resilient spirit, a certain faith that life has meaning, and an absolutely superb therapist with whom I explored dark places and early sorrows. If, as Plato says, "the unexamined life is not worth living," then, I believe, the corollary is also true: the examined life *is* worth living.

I do not believe these changes would have happened had Frank not been in my life. However brief our time together, it changed me forever. I grew up, a Depression-era child, whom my parents did not want. My first husband probably loved me as well as he could, but his heart was in his scholarly studies and not with me. I needed the unqualified love of a good man to become a complete person. It was the foundation of a new life.

The life I have so much enjoyed living does not sound very exciting on the face of it. True, there are some exciting stories from my travels during my fifties and sixties. I explored much of Italy, cruised the Greek Islands, rode a camel in Egypt and an elephant in India, was mugged and robbed in Nairobi, and made a fool of myself trying to use chopsticks in a restaurant in Beijing.

Most of my adventures, though, are quieter ones. I savor the miracles of everyday life—the pileated woodpecker at my bird feeder, a good talk with my son Dan, discovering a new poet or short-story writer, a friend's instinctive understanding of something I haven't yet said.

The great pleasure I have always found in music, art, and poetry has grown more intense with age. Perhaps that is because Bach and Rembrandt and Keats are old friends now, familiar but still able to delight. Perhaps I see things now that I missed when I was younger.

I don't mean to suggest that I expect to escape the problems of growing old alone. Of course I will not. Sometimes I am lonely, but loneliness is not the same as emptiness. It is just part of the human condition and has to be accepted. So it is with various other aches and pains and shortcomings of old age. They have to be put up with; but as long as they are not interfering too much, I try to get on with my life and not wear out my friends' patience by grizzling about them.

After Frank died, I started going to church. I had no creed or set of beliefs. I simply wanted to join a church as a way of acknowledging some deep, inner changes and perhaps of finding a setting in which they could grow. I could have joined anything, but I chose the Episcopal Church, partly because Aunt Pearl, whom I loved, had been a member and partly because I had found a beautiful old Episcopal church off Lafayette Square in Washington, D.C. and had come to love the poetry of *The Book of Common Prayer*.

I have remained a church-goer ever since. I find the ancient liturgy moving and I enjoy the companionship of the church community. I am not concerned with finding literal "truth": I regard many of the traditional ideas as myths which, like art and music and poetry, express what ordinary words cannot. My faith, if that is the word, is that whatever helps us live more fully and more compassionately is "true." "I know I shall not know," T. S. Eliot says in *Ash Wednesday*. That is how I feel—and I am at peace with the mystery.

I believe I am at last the person I was meant to be. That is a huge achievement. I am old now, but I do not feel diminished by age.

I hope I have another decade as pleasant as the last one has been, but if not, then not. I intend to celebrate every day and not waste precious time looking back with regret or forward with fear.

I am aware that at my age, 83, death is a kind of next-door neighbor. Having watched Frank die, I can never forget how something happened at the end to grace his passing. Just what happened remains a mystery, but the memory is comforting.

Epilogue

I always would have preferred to go through life with Frank at my side, but he would have been pleased to know how I lived my life. I still think of him almost every day; and while I do not so much mind going through the difficult times alone, I often think how much better he would have made the good ones. Sometimes when a hawk or an egret or a goldfinch flies very near, I think Frank has sent him my way to say hello. Then I remember that whenever Frank sent a message, he always closed it with the words, "Be of good cheer."

I am of good cheer, Frank. I really am.